THE MASS

THE MASS
Finding Its Meaning for You— And Getting More Out of It

Gerard P. Weber

*I am most grateful for the help and suggestions
of Irene Murphy, James Comiskey and Cullen Schippe,
and for the faithful service of my Epson computer.*

Nihil Obstat: Rev. Thomas Richstatter, O.F.M.
  Rev. John J. Jennings

Imprimi Potest: Rev. Jeremy Harrington, O.F.M.
  Provincial

Imprimatur: + James H. Garland, V.G.
  Archdiocese of Cincinnati
  May 2, 1985

The *nihil obstat* and *imprimatur* are a declaration that a book or pamphlet is considered to be free from doctrinal or moral error. It is not implied that those who have granted the *nihil obstat* and *imprimatur* agree with the contents, opinions or statements expressed.

Scripture texts used in this work are taken from the *New American Bible*, copyright ©1970 by the Confraternity of Christian Doctrine, Washington, D.C., and are used by permission of the copyright owner. All rights reserved.

The selection from *Orthodoxy* by G. K. Chesterton is reprinted with permission of the publisher, Dodd, Mead & Company, Inc., New York, N.Y.

The selection by Tad Guzie is reprinted from *Chicago Studies*, Vol. 22, no. 3 (November), "Salvation III—Sign & Sacrament," and is reprinted with permission.

Book design and cover by Julie Lonneman.

SBN 0-86716-049-7

Contents

Contents

Introduction

One sentiment surfaces time and time again when I talk about the Mass with teenagers, young adults, mature adults and even senior citizens. In a dozen different ways they all seem to say, "It's boring!"

Occasional disappointment can't be avoided. And we certainly can't expect a peak experience every time we gather for Eucharist. But a habitual attitude that the Mass is a burden, that little or nothing of what is happening is of interest, is a serious religious problem.

I must admit that for many years I thought the antidote for that boredom was *learning more about* the Eucharist. But as I become more and more conscious of how often *I* am bored when celebrating Mass, I realize the antidote lies someplace else. Beautiful, logical and inspiring explanations of the meaning of the Mass have little or no impact on how I participate at the Eucharist. But I find that tedium very often disappears when I seriously ask—and answer—the question, "What's in it for me?"

This book is designed to raise that same question for you—and to help you answer it by asking a further question, "What do I *hope* to get out of the Mass?" When I ask those two questions of myself and answer them honestly, two things usually happen.

First, I begin to question *my* motives and no longer blame "them," whoever the "them" might be, for failing to create a more interesting liturgy. This helps me take responsibility for interesting myself in the Mass. I compare my motives for participating with the insights the Church has accumulated over the centuries to see what stronger motives might be hidden in this collected wisdom. Often this process suggests motives which I had not seriously explored before.

Second, asking those questions helps me clarify what I want out of Mass. Then I can try to do what is in my power to lead a liturgy which will satisfy my need. Laypeople can, of course, set off on a search for a parish with the type of liturgy which meets their needs.

But these two questions can have an even greater effect: They lead me to reflect on what Jesus intended for his followers when he said, "Do this in memory of me," and on why the saints and the great Christians of all ages have found such strength and consolation in the Eucharist.

This book is for people who have been going to Mass for years, who at times feel bored, but who really *want* to get something from the Mass. The desire to learn is the first and most important step in acquiring knowledge. So, too, wanting to get something out of the Mass is the first and most important step in overcoming boredom.

The book is not a scholarly exposition on the Mass. It does not build one idea upon another or tell you what you "should" know. It does not outline all the motives for participating in the Eucharist or all the benefits to be gained from that practice. It does help you explore *your* motives and what you hope to get from Mass. It also offers some practical suggestions which may help you in overcoming boredom.

The Plan of Action

This book is divided into three parts. Part One gives us a chance to get acquainted with one another, to discover who we are as we gather to celebrate the Eucharist and what responsibility each of us has for making the liturgy a satisfying celebration. Part Two explores the most common reasons people give for attending Mass. It is intended to help you clarify *your* motives for being there and, in the process, clarify the expectations you bring with you. Part Three sketches some practical steps toward getting more out of the Mass.

In each chapter I share some of my personal experience and reflection. Questions at the end of each chapter invite you to explore your own experience; there is room on those pages to jot down a few notes. Perhaps you will want to share your reflection with others. I would, in fact, recommend using this book with a small group of friends or fellow parishioners, or even with the adult members of your family.

The book will be most helpful, I believe, if you do *not* read it straight through. Rather, take it one chapter at a time, reflect on the questions, share your answers with others, and then put the book down and come back to it in a few days.

Someone has said that we learn as little as possible about what we *have* to know, nothing at all about what other people tell us we *should* know, and as much as possible about what we *want* to know. The truth of this statement hit me when I bought my computer.

The salesman demonstrated many of the capabilities of the machine and gave me four programs besides the one I wanted for word processing. He felt I *had to know* about these programs in order to appreciate my computer. I have never used these four programs because I have no need for them. My mailing list is small; my bookkeeping is all done in the checkbook; I have no interest in electronic mail; and I don't like to play computer games.

A close friend has been trying to get me to learn what I *should know* about how a computer works so I can do all sorts of wonderful things. But I don't care *how* it works as long as it *does* work when I punch a key. I politely ignore all that he says.

In contrast, a teacher gave me several hours of instructions on what I *wanted to know* about word processing. I didn't understand half of what he said, but it was a start in learning how to use the machine. I read the manual, launched many trials and made a few errors. Gradually I understood what I had to do to accomplish what I wanted, and I really don't care about the rest. I hope you will use this book in the same way.

I hope this book will be at least as useful to you as the one cooking lesson I had. Off and on for years I have made my own breakfast. Never once have I scrambled an egg properly or managed to turn one over lightly without breaking the yolk. I do not know how to cook, and I really do not care to learn.

But one day I watched a friend prepare bourbon steak. I was intrigued with how simple it was: Pan-fry a steak and smother it with a delicious flaming sauce of mushrooms, olives, onions, pimento, butter and whiskey. A week or so later I tried my hand and made a tolerable bourbon steak.

One success does not make me a chef. But now I appreciate much more what goes into preparing a good meal and I am much more interested in cooking. Some day I may even learn to make eggs Benedict!

So, if what is in the book is helpful, together we can thank God. If it is not, at least some basic questions have been raised.

Gerard P. Weber
Encino, California
September, 1984

PART ONE

Laying the Groundwork

CHAPTER ONE

Faces Around the Table:
Introducing Ourselves

One morning I was substituting for a priest who was away caring for his dying father. I got to the church early and waited for someone to show up and tell me how things were done at that parish. A thin, spry, well-dressed man appeared and introduced himself: "I'm Sam. I open the church every morning and help distribute Communion."

He went on to tell me that he was 72 years old and that he had been going to Mass every day for the past 15 years. He was so warm and open I had no fear of asking him, "Sam, did you go to Mass every Sunday when you were younger?"

He shook his head and said, "Father, you know how it is when you are young." Indeed I did know. But I was curious as to why he now went to Mass every day, so I asked him. His answer was short and to the point, "I'm a Catholic."

"What's that got to do with it?" I asked in surprise.

"You know," he said, "everyone's got a job to do. I always believed in doing my job well. Bricklayers lay brick. Painters paint. Catholics go to Mass."

Sam's response was not a very profound theological reason for participating in the Eucharist on Sunday, much less every day. But somehow he sensed that there was something very important in the Mass for him.

Each of us, like Sam, has personal reasons for participating (or not participating) in the Eucharist. Together, let's look into these reasons and learn from them what we *expect* to get out of the Mass. Then we can ask what we actually *do* get out of joining in the Eucharistic celebration, and what we can do to fill our expectations. But, first, let's get acquainted.

Introducing the Author

I have been a priest for 40 years. After 25 years of parish work, I am now resident chaplain in a retreat center. I am not particularly pious and my daily struggle, like that of all Christians, is to "put on Christ" a little more each day. I seldom ask myself more than three times a week, "What can I do to make the Eucharist a little more meaningful for myself and for those celebrating with me?"

Who Are You?

Now, who are you, the reader? I presume that you are Catholic and that you go to Mass, at least occasionally. From what I observe from the altar, I would guess that you fall into one of three general categories: the spectators, the loners, the participators. Of course everyone is a bit of each, but on the whole each person will have a tendency to be more one than the other two. Particular needs at a particular time in life will cause a person to favor one mode over another.

If we reflect for a moment about how people engage in sports we will better understand the meaning of these categories. A great many people who never go onto a playing field love to watch sports. Monday night football on TV has become an American tradition. Forty million people paid to watch baseball games last year; 100,000 sat in the stands at a single football game.

These attendance figures prove that people get something out of watching sports. Not all the spectators, of course, derive the same enjoyment from watching a game. Those with a knowledge of the game's subtleties and a commitment to the home team obviously enjoy the game more than those who are merely watching it to pass the time. But none of them need do the hard work of getting in shape, practicing and actually playing. Spectators sit back with beer and hot dogs and enjoy what the trained athletes are doing out on the field.

A great many people also engage in sports. Some prefer playing on a team, while others enjoy sports which one can do

8

alone. Football, baseball, tennis, volleyball and bridge are no fun if one tries to play by oneself. Horseback riding, running, fishing and hunting are better sports for solitary players.

Players who have to depend on the other members of the team to win need skills which the solitary player does not need. A quarterback who is as silent as a trout fisherman would be a disaster on the football field.

Why this seeming digression on sports? The same three types of people sit in the pews on Sunday.

There are the *spectators* who may know a great deal or very little about the nature of the Mass, but like to watch a good performance by the priest, the readers, the preacher and the choir. If any or all of these people do poorly, the spectators feel that they are not getting as much as they should out of the Mass.

Then there are the *loners*, the solitary players who love the Mass as a time for their own personal prayer—a time to say the rosary, read a prayer book or quietly meditate. They want the choir to be unobtrusive, the homilist to be short and the celebrant to do his thing without disturbing them. They get the most out of Mass when the choir, the celebrant and the congregation (no crying babies, please!) provide a restful, quiet time for prayer. Before Vatican II 80 to 90 percent of the people at Mass prayed in this solitary fashion.

Finally, there are the *participators*. They get most out of the Mass when they experience a sense of unity with the celebrant and the rest of the congregation. They enjoy singing aloud, praying together, giving the handshake of peace. The homily is important to them because they want a message for their lives, and they are willing to listen with attention to what the speaker is saying.

All of us need to be spectators at times because nothing is going on in our lives which we can relate to the Mass. At other times we need to be loners because so much is going on that we need to pray and reflect quietly. I would guess that at every Mass most of us, celebrant included, are a little bit spectator and a little bit loner. But, if I may be excused for using the comparison, the Mass is a *team sport*.

The Mass requires all of us, priest and people, to be actively involved. We each have our own particular and important role. I, as a priest, should not perform all the roles. Just as no one person can play all the positions on a baseball team so, too, the Eucharist requires a division of labor. All the people in Church are called to perform their individual roles in interaction with one another, to be conscious that they are part of a community, that they are doing Eucharist together. Merely "being at" the liturgy is not enough.

Who Are We?

I have told you a bit about myself and a bit about who I think you are. The question then arises, "Who are *we* when we get together to celebrate Mass?" We are a community of Catholics who, on Sunday (and sometimes during the week), sit at the Lord's table to share fellowship with Jesus and those present with us. Eating together is a sign of our unity, of our acceptance of one another and of our friendship.

I must honestly admit that I do not often feel this unity, acceptance and friendship when I celebrate Mass in a large parish or when I visit a parish I have never been to before. But in spite of my very real difficulty in experiencing this unity, I do *believe* that you and I are united in a very special way when we gather to celebrate the Lord's Supper. We usually do not invite enemies to our home for a meal. If we invite strangers, we do so that they may no longer be strangers but become acquaintances and even friends.

I am one of those people who have a hard time remembering people's names and getting to know them. (I guess I am basically an introvert and a bit shy.) When I became a pastor I decided to try to get to know the parishioners. Each month I invited 10 or 12 people in for Saturday-night Kentucky Fried Chicken. The only purpose of the supper was to get to know one another a little better. I issued the invitation to the entire parish and asked people to sign up if they would like to come to this little get-together. If I remember correctly, only about 10 percent of the parish had dinner with me and some of the staff members. (I do remember growing awfully tired of fried chicken and soggy fries.) But those who came did get to know me, the staff and each other a little better.

Eating together is more than sitting at the same table consuming food. When we go to a friend's house we don't place our meal on a TV tray and sit off in a corner absorbed in our own thoughts or watching what is going on. We join in the conversation and festivities as well as in the eating and drinking. When we come to church we are at a meal with friends, and we should all join in the celebration.

People often think of the early Christian community as a group of followers of Jesus characterized only by love: "See how these Christians love one another!" But St. Luke says that their common identity was also manifested by the fact that they ate together:

> They devoted themselves to the apostles' instruction and the communal life, *to the breaking of the bread and the prayers*....Those who believed shared all things in common; they would sell their property and goods, dividing everything on the basis of each one's need. They went to the temple area together every day, while *in their homes they broke bread. With exultant and sincere hearts they took their meals in common.*" (Acts 2:42, 44-46, emphases added)

In this idealistic picture of the first converts we hear a description of who *we* are. We are a people who listen to the message of Jesus transmitted to us through our leaders; we are a people who share with those in need; we are a people who pray together; and we are a people who break bread together—St. Luke's way of saying we celebrate the Lord's Supper. This is the identity you and I reaffirm each time we celebrate the Eucharist.

At Table With Jesus

It was not by accident that St. Luke described the first Christians as people who broke bread together. He was rounding out one of the motifs which run through his Gospel. Many times he tells that Jesus ate with various people, and each of these meals highlights in dramatic form one or more of the characteristics expected of those who strive to be his disciples.

Each of these stories tells us something of who we are, and of what we, as Christians, are expected to try to be if we participate in the Eucharist. Let's take a quick look at those stories to see what they suggest to us about the kind of people we are called to be when we assemble at the table of the Lord:

—The first recorded meal with Jesus was at the house of Levi, the tax collector (Luke 5:27-39). Everyone at the table was a social outcast, a sinner—Levi's friends and co-workers—but they were all welcome. Jesus was not picky about who sat at the table with him.

—When the "town scandal" interrupted dinner at the home of Simon the Pharisee (Luke 7:37-50), Jesus made it clear that forgiveness was extended and experienced at that meal because of her love.

—We often forget that Jesus himself must have eaten with the crowd at the multiplication of the loaves (Luke 9:10-17). The disciples had just returned from their first preaching journey, and Jesus gave them a mission to reach out to the hungry and feed them.

—The delightful story of dinner at the home of Martha and Mary (Luke 10:38-42) highlights the fact that the externals of the celebration, of the festivities, are not nearly as important as being concerned about the guests and being open to hearing the word of the Lord.

—Next Luke records two dinners at the homes of Pharisees. In one Jesus stresses interior attitudes over external observance (Luke 11:37-54), and in the other the need for humility and willingness to take the lowest place (Luke 14:1-24).

—The man of short stature, the tax collector Zacchaeus, was so full of gratitude when Christ invited himself for dinner that he gave half his goods to the poor (Luke 19:1-10).

—In his short account of the Last Supper, Luke makes the kind of love Jesus had for his friends clear in Jesus' promise to shed his blood for them (Luke 22:13-35).

—The last time the risen Lord ate with his friends he gave them the greatest of all gifts, peace (Luke 24:35-39).

There are many other elements in these stories, of course. But as we read them a picture gradually emerges of the atmosphere in which the Eucharist should be celebrated. We who gather have been called to follow Jesus, no matter what our past lives have been. Each time we gather we hear his call to change our lives and our way of thinking, and we have the opportunity to respond to him. It is not the external ceremonies which count as much as the interior dispositions of our hearts:

love, openness to all people, unconditional forgiveness, reconciliation, generosity to the poor, service to others and willingness to suffer for them. The great gift we are offered is peace. The Gospel picture of meal is idealistic, but ideals are important because they picture what might be and inspire us to try to make them real.

We Are Catholic Christians

When I celebrate the Eucharist, I usually am conscious that I am doing something specifically *Catholic*. Eucharist not only reminds me that I am a Christian trying to live a Gospel life, but also that I am a Catholic who puts the breaking of the bread, the sharing at the Lord's table, the Mass as the focal point of my life from which all other things should flow. My identity comes not only from listening to and accepting the Word of the Lord; it comes also from daily breaking bread in memory of him.

All four Gospel writers show that Jesus' last meal was not only the hour which he had looked forward to with longing but also an hour which belonged in a most special way to his followers. When Jesus told them, "Do this as a remembrance of me" (Luke 22:19), he was asking them—and through them, us—to take on the attitude and commitment he was to show in his final confrontation with the powers of darkness.

When you and I gather for the breaking of the bread and do what Jesus did, we are expressing our commitment to do the will of the Father, to trust the Father in all circumstances, to face down the power of evil in us and around us and to serve one another.

If we read the fuller expression of Jesus' attitude and commitment in John 14—17, we will know who we are called to be. We are friends, servants of one another, brothers and sisters of Jesus and of each other, children of a loving Father. Each Eucharist is a birthday party at which we give thanks for the common life we have and at which we affirm and proclaim our identity as Christians who are Catholic.

For Reflection and Sharing

1) I have told you a bit about myself. If I were present, what would you tell me about:
    a) How you usually participate at Mass?

    b) How you feel at Mass?

    c) How frequently you attend Mass?

    d) What the Mass means to you?

2) Recall a time when you were a spectator at Mass.
    a) Why did you feel like a spectator?

    b) What benefit did you get from being a spectator?

3) Recall a time when you were a loner at Mass.
    a) Why did you want to be a loner?

    b) What benefit did you get from being a loner?

4) Recall a time when you really felt like a participator.
    a) Why did you feel that you were really participating?

    b) What benefit did you get from being a participator?

5) The Mass is a ritual meal done in memory of Jesus. Read all four Gospel accounts of the Last Supper (Matthew 26:20-35; Mark 14:12-31; Luke 22:14-38; John 13—17) and pick out two or three qualities mentioned or alluded to which you think should characterize a person who shares in table fellowship with Jesus and the Christian community.

6) Consider how these qualities are found in your own life or in the life of your parish. How might they become more obvious in your personal life? In the life of your parish?

CHAPTER TWO

Let's Get Our Act Together: Sharing Responsibility for the Mass

When I began to think about this book I did some comsumer research. I asked my good friend Jim what he thought people could do to get more out of the Mass. His response was vehement: "What can *we* do? All I've heard is what *we* should do! I'm tired of hearing that! Let the *priests* get their act together!" A few days later he called me back. He had done some consumer research on his own; he had taken my question to six friends. The response was unanimous: "Let the priests get their act together!"

This very scientific and comprehensive piece of research raised several questions for me. First, "Whose 'act' is the Mass?"

There is no doubt that in pre-Vatican II days people looked upon the Mass as the priest's action. He did something up there at the altar; they watched and perhaps said some prayers. To see how deeply and how long this attitude has infected the Catholic mentality we have only to look at our church buildings.

The great cathedrals of the past and most of the churches built before 1960 were designed to emphasize the role of the priest. They usually were rectangular in shape with long rows of pews stretching far back into the church. In some of the famous cathedrals the sanctuary was almost completely shut off from the view of the people by choir stalls, screens or gratings. The priest functioned on an elevated platform with his back to the people. The sanctuary, set off by an altar rail, was always well lighted, while the people often sat in semi-darkness. The most beautiful and powerful decorations centered on the sanctuary while the main body of the church was frequently very plain.

The priest alone was allowed to speak in Church. The laity were expected to be silent, at most joining in an occasional hymn. Many years ago a wag said that the laity had three roles at Mass: to kneel in silence at prayer, to sit and listen in silence to the sermon and to open their pocketbooks and silently contribute to the collection.

Even in those dark days of nonparticipation, canon law directed that a priest could not offer Mass without at least a server present—even if that server happened to be another priest. That law protected the belief that Mass was for and with the community of faithful; the server was the token representative of the congregation.

At least 75 years before Pope John XXIII called the Second Vatican Council, voices were raised calling for more lay participation. The gentle, almost imperceptible whispers of the liturgical pioneers of the late 19th and early 20th centuries gradually grew in strength and volume until in 1963 they reached gale force in the Council's first decree, *The Constitution on the Sacred Liturgy*. The bishops said, "Christ's faithful, when present at this mystery of faith should not be there as strangers or silent spectators. On the contrary, through a proper appreciation of the rites and prayers they should participate knowingly, devoutly and actively" (#48).

The Constitution on the Sacred Liturgy provides the official answer of the Church to the question, "Whose 'act' is the Mass?" It belongs to all of us!

As a result of that decree we now have active participation in the prayers of the Mass, lay ministers, communal singing and liturgy committees. We also have new churches whose very stones shout whose action the Mass is. Whether or not we like them, whether or not they are great works of architecture, we have to admit that our new buildings are designed for interaction between priest and people. Many new churches are so arranged that no one sits more than 10 pews away from the altar, which itself is no longer high above or far away from the people. A few new churches further emphasize community by enlarging the entrance hall so people can mingle before and after Mass.

Although the Eucharist is the celebration of the entire community, the priest still hold a central role. He is the one who

18

pulls it together, orchestrates it and gives it feeling and tone, much like the conductor of a symphony orchestra. But without the cooperation and active, intense participation of the rest of the ministers and the entire congregation, the priest's efforts will be in vain.

The Congregation's Role

The second question raised by my research is this: "What are the people in the pews actually feeling and thinking?" When I stand at the altar on Sunday and look at the congregation, I see a good many people who seem genuinely interested in what is going on. Their attitude seems to be, "We are here to pray with you and with each other." I feel encouraged by what I see and I try to pray in a way that invites them to join me in praising the Lord.

I also see many people who do not seem so interested— who, indeed, seem downright bored. I ask myself what they are thinking and feeling, why they are here. Some are children who squirm and fidget; their restlessness I can understand. Others are teenagers who read the bulletin, flip through the song book or talk out of the side of their mouths without moving their lips. I can remember back far enough to sympathize with their boredom.

I have more trouble understanding the blank-faced adults. I think of some good friends who were bored for years, yet went to Mass every Sunday "for the sake of the children." Most of them gave up before they overcame their tedium. I am curious about those who slouch in the pew, the people whose body language says, "I dare you to involve me." These are people who challenge me to move and speak and gesture in a way that will catch their attention.

The celebrant, the choir, the liturgy planners can all work to make the Mass alive and interesting. And well-conducted and innovative liturgies will at times push back the threshold of boredom. Nevertheless, we can't expect Fourth of July fireworks every Sunday. The lasting antidote for boredom must come from what the participants themselves feel, think and do.

A person who begins to see what is occurring at Mass as personally meaningful will no longer be bored. This new way of seeing, however, has to come from the heart, not the head.

It has to be knowledge reflected upon, prayed over and made part of one's whole being.

There are many avenues a person can explore to find a new perspective on the Eucharist. Participating in a prayer group, sharing ideas and experiences in small groups, listening to talks, reading books, studying the Scriptures, private prayer, making the effort to establish ties with other people in the parish—all these help to give a different perspective and to reduce the threshold of boredom.

The Priest's Role

My third question is this: "Why don't priests do a better job as celebrants?"

Most priests I know agree in principle with the ideas contained in *The Constitution on the Liturgy*. But, like all human beings, they have selective memories of what is called for and sometimes have difficulty recognizing the implications for their own actions. They may accept the concept that the Mass is a communal action of the People of God, but resent laypeople (especially women) "mucking around" in the sanctuary. They may turn the altar around to face the people but still say the prayers as if they alone were talking to God.

One day I concelebrated with a good friend of mine. Not once did he look at the people or use his voice to draw them in. His gestures were stilted, his voice muted and monotonous. Afterwards I commented that he wasn't communicating very well with the congregation. His reaction surprised me: "I'm talking to God, not to the people out there. He hears what I'm saying." Obviously he had not thought through the implications of the idea that he was the leader of the people's prayer, called to preside and give order to *their* celebration.

I often find that priests with all the goodwill in the world just do not know how to give life to a celebration. This is not always the individual's fault. The books they have read and the conferences they have attended have been long on ideals and principles and short on demonstrations of how to be a good presider and how to use the options the liturgy allows to enhance the particular occasion. Not everyone is creative.

Finally, I suspect that some priests are mediocre celebrants because they have fallen into routine or because the

Mass has become a duty or a burden. I remember how difficult it was for me to muster up enthusiasm for Sunday the last year I was in a parish. The moment I stepped out of the rectory my stomach turned, and it churned till the last Mass was over. Part of my problem was physical, but a greater part was that I was bored and discouraged—burned out, in modern jargon. Thank the Lord, I can once again muster up real enthusiasm for preaching and celebrating.

Many priests are, of course, very fine leaders of prayer who involve the people and communicate a sense that the Eucharist is really a communal action. I myself sometimes do a good job. At other times I know that I do not have my act together. In answering this question, I may sound like a I am apologizing for my brethren. Actually, I am asking for understanding. The man at the altar is just that—a man, a human being.

My friend Jim comprehends the human factor. He does not, however, accept these explanations as reasonable excuses. He feels that more effort should be directed toward educating the clergy.

But most dioceses already have an office of continuing education for priests that offers conferences and opportunities for updating and renewal. I do not think that more talks and more conferences will help a whole lot. Perhaps what priests really need are more opportunities to surface, examine and reevaluate their attitudes toward their role and the role of laypeople not only at Mass but in the entire life and functioning of the Church.

Taking Responsibility

There is not much ordinary laypersons can do to foster the continuing education of priests. But they can do much to help a priest change his attitudes. If the congregation has a difficult time when the celebrant is apathetic and bored, the reverse is equally true. The celebrant has just as difficult a time when he senses the people are apathetic, bored and even resistant to what he is doing. But when a man knows that his efforts are appreciated—especially when he knows *which* efforts are appreciated—he is spurred to better achievements. We all want to be liked and appreciated.

21

Recently I concelebrated the funeral Mass of an old friend. The pastor, well into his 70's, rattled off the prayers in a singsong voice, but he made an effort to include the man's name in practically every prayer he said. He had prepared a sermon which was very personal and touching. Later the family told *me* how much they appreciated that Mass and what the pastor said and did—but they neglected to tell the man who did it.

When, Sunday after Sunday, I stand outside the church after Mass and hear not one comment on the homily, I feel that the people do not care—so why should I? When someone says that I gave a good sermon and mentions how a specific point touched home, I am encouraged to try to be at least as specific the next time I preach.

Negative comments help most when they come from a trusted friend. In my early years I was a great hell-fire preacher, usually because I was not prepared. One day a close friend told me how much my talks disturbed her because they were so negative and condemnatory. I took her remarks to heart, and it has been a long time since I stoked the fires of hell from the pulpit. Another friend sat in the third pew and kept track on his fingers of grammatical mistakes and slang expressions. My eyes were on his fingers a good part of the time, but I did clean up my act.

Where attitudes and practices change slowly, perhaps the most Christian thing to do is to recite a version of the Serenity Prayer before each Mass: "God grant me the serenity to accept the things I cannot change about the priest, the choir, the organist, the other people in the parish. Give me the courage to change the things I can about my attitude toward the Mass, my understanding of it, my participation in it. Finally, grant me the wisdom to know what falls under my responsibility and what is someone else's responsibility."

For Reflection and Sharing

1) Take a little time to visit your parish church or to picture it in your imagination. What do the physical structure and the appointments of the church suggest to you about the role of the priest, the role of laypeople, the role of priest and people acting together?

—the position of the altar

—the position of the priest's chair

—the presence or absence of an altar rail

—the size of the sanctuary

—the arrangement of the pews

—the placement of the organ

—the placement of the choir

—the lighting in the church

—the decorations in the church

—the availability of song books

2) Take a few minutes to picture what happens in your church. Evaluate whether or not what is said and done conveys the message that this is the action of all the People of God.

—How well do the people join in the singing?

—How well do the people answer the prayers?

—How many lay ministers usually participate?

—Is the sign of peace merely a token gesture or is it a real greeting?

—Do you have the feeling that your presence, actions and prayers really contribute something to the celebration of the Eucharist?

3) How would you describe your own attitude when you go to Mass? The attitude of the people around you?

4) What does the priest convey to you by his gestures, bodily movements, tone of voice?
—That the Mass is his action and his alone?

—That he tolerates the participation of the laity?

—That he is leading an activity in which all the people participate in varying degrees?

5) When was the last time you complimented a priest on his sermon or leadership of prayer by mentioning one specific thing that touched you? What was his reaction? If you have not done this, what has held you back?

How would you describe your attitude and feeling about each of the priests in the parish? If your attitude is positive and appreciative, how have you expressed it to the priests?

6) If you have frequently felt boredom at Mass, what have you done to overcome that boredom?

CHAPTER THREE

When the Ground Shifts: Changing Expectations of the Mass

$\mathbf{I}$ must admit I have a hidden agenda in writing this book. I, too, am searching for an answer to the question, "Why should I go to Mass?" Before I can formulate an answer to that question I think I have to ask two other questions. The first is, "Why do I celebrate Mass today?" The second is, "Why have I gone to Mass in the past?"

I find it rather difficult to give my reasons for celebrating Mass today because they seem to conflict with each other. Some mornings when I feel alive and well, I really want to celebrate with the community. Other mornings when I can barely get out of bed for the 7:45 Mass, I am there because the people expect me to be there. Some Sundays saying one Mass is a chore. Other Sundays I will help out with a second Mass at a small black parish because I enjoy being with the people and hearing the choir sing with soul. Once in a while the profound theological meaning of what I am doing will motivate me to step onto the altar. At other times a pressing need or worry will make me want to be with the Lord.

I honestly cannot say that I have one motive—not even a predominant motive. I do not know what motivates you, but I would guess that faith, habit, fear, inertia, social pressure, deep conviction and a host of other more personal reasons prompt you to build the Eucharist into your Sunday schedule.

I find the answer to the second question—why I have gone to Mass over the years—most intriguing. It was not until I began to write this book that I reflected on the changes which

25

have occurred in my motivation and on the process by which those changes took place.

A Bit of Personal History

I went to a public school. As far as I can remember I never went to a weekday Mass but never missed a Sunday. It was taken for granted in our family that the first thing we did on Sunday morning was go to Mass—no arguments, no discussion, no questioning.

When I entered the junior (high school) seminary, the spiritual director told us that seminarians were expected to go to Mass every morning. A person who obeyed my superiors, I got up every morning for five years, ran down the block for the 7 a.m. Mass, dashed home for a bowl of cereal and hopped on the bus for the seminary. I didn't ask why. It was expected of me. It was what I was supposed to do if I wanted to be a good priest—and I wanted to be a priest, hopefully a good one!

The English daily Missal was just coming into widespread use at the time. Before then, prayer books had a section of prayers to say at Mass. But now I could say the same prayers the priest said. I knew that I *really* prayed each morning because I read the official prayers of the Church. I felt good about myself, about my efforts to pray and about being at Mass each day.

When we went to the major seminary, the great liturgist Monsignor Reynold Hillenbrand was rector. He did all in his power, from inspiring talks to well-executed liturgies, to help us become participators. He explained the "what" and the "how" of the Mass clearly and compellingly. He was, in effect, giving us reasons for going to Mass, hoping that his reasons would become our reasons.

But at that time I was not even asking the question *why*. And no one on the faculty raised it for me. We were *expected* to be at Mass and meditation every day. Once or twice I slept through the rising bell; and five minutes after the end of Mass, the disciplinarian was knocking at my door to find out if I was sick. During those years I studied many theories of Eucharist and learned the reasons why people should attend daily if possible. I tried to make them my own.

I became very interested in the liturgical movement and saw in it the solution for all the problems of the Church and the world (well, maybe not *all*, but most). The Church expected Mass, meditation, rosary, daily visits and prayer of its priests; that unspoken assumption always overcame any reluctance I felt about rolling out of bed for chapel at 6 a.m.

When I was ordained I frequently preached on the nature of the Mass, urged people to receive Communion every Sunday, attended liturgical conferences and conducted classes on the liturgy. For the 30 years I was in a parish the personal *why* never bothered me because there was no question about my being at daily Mass. I had a schedule of Mass intentions and stipends. There were always people waiting for me to come to the altar. If the love of God and a desire for sanctity did not draw me there, a deep sense of responsibility did. I knew what was expected of me, and I was willing and glad to assume that responsibility.

For 25 of those 30 years I took it for granted that my priest friends and I would say Mass every day on vacation, no matter how difficult it was to find a church or to find a proper place to set up our portable altar. During these years I was sure that offering the sacrifice of the Mass and receiving Communion was the primary way for a Catholic to get closer to God. (Whether or not I did get closer to him through those 10,000 Masses will not be known until Judgment Day.)

Then two different events occurred which cracked the way I had thought about the Mass for 35 years. First, Vatican II made official the changes in the liturgy which I had always felt would usher in a golden age, changes which I thought would raise the percentage of Catholics going to Mass every Sunday from 70 to 90 and bring as many as a fourth of the parishioners to daily Mass. The rite was reformed; the liturgical seasons were given their proper emphasis; fasting rules were eased; concelebration was reintroduced; and, best of all, Latin was replaced by English. All the things we had only dreamed of in the 1940's and 50's were now possible in the 60's and 70's.

What has actually happened? People did start going to Communion more often. In fact, in most parishes practically everyone receives—those living in "meaningful relationships," those who miss more Masses than they attend, some of the good Protestants who happen to be present, many of the divorced and remarried. The definition of who is "worthy" to receive Communion certainly has been rewritten by the practice of the people in the pews.

But Mass attendance has declined perceptibly. In my parish our Sunday head count fell from 900 to 600 in four years—in spite of the fact that the 900 represented at best 50 percent of the baptized Catholics living in the parish. As I watched what was happening I began to question whether the reasons we had been giving for attending Mass were really as compelling as we thought they were. I began to ask myself about *my* reasons for participating in the liturgy. For the first time, I was not thinking about liturgical theories of the Mass or Church expectations, but about my own conviction and needs.

The second event which helped to change my thinking on the Mass was a bout of colitis. I resigned my pastorate in order to rest, and I took lodging in a seminary where I had no responsibility for Sunday or weekday Mass. For the first time there was no subtle, unspoken, not-quite-conscious expectation that I would go to the altar of God each day. In this quiet, peaceful, reflective atmosphere I struggled for months not only with the question, "Why the Mass?" but also with the question, "What is this priesthood if I do not hear confessions each Saturday and celebrate Mass every day?"

After a time, I settled the question of what it means to be a priest in a way which is satisfactory to me in my present situation as a resident chaplain in a retreat center. But the first question—Why the Mass?—still is not entirely settled.

'They' Are Not the Answer

Like most people, I would like to find a magic formula that would make the Eucharist more meaningful for me and for those who celebrate with me. Here at the retreat center I see the sisters and novices in residence struggling to make daily Eucharist and the celebration of important feasts really relevant to us. Some of the things they do speak to me; many leave me cold. But by now I am convinced that I cannot look to others to make the Eucharistic celebration relevant and meaningful in my life. There is little "they" can do to make it the center of my day.

A solemn ceremony with choir, orchestra and wonderful decorations may stir me and put me into a reverential mood—but who can stand such a rich diet every day or even every week?

A good homily, whether I hear it or prepare it, will inspire me—but who can prepare such homilies day after day, week after week? A well-planned, innovative liturgy often intrigues me and involves me—but one can take only so many balloons, clowns, banners or pageants.

I am beginning to see very clearly that the Mass makes sense and is important not only because of what is being done in the church, but also because of what is going on in my life. My experiences, my troubles, my successes, my failures as a person and as a priest are what give importance to the fact that we are gathered at a banquet table to offer once again the sacrifice of the death, resurrection and ascension of Jesus. Finally I am beginning to realize that *my* approach to the Mass is not the only one—or even the best one.

The logical side of my brain dominates my life. Things have to make sense to me. I am most comfortable expressing myself verbally. Therefore, I am most at ease in a church that is rather plain, without pictures and statues. I like to stand near the first pew so I can informally share my ideas with the people. Music, drama, dance, banners, pageants and carefully executed rituals make little impression on me most of the time. But I have discovered that they do make a powerful impression on people in whom the artistic side of the brain is very active and influential

Parishes which offer a variety of Masses every weekend are very wise. Some people need quiet; others prefer a folk Mass, or a charismatic celebration, or a Mass with a large choir singing classical music.

The Process of Change

Before we go any further, let me outline the steps I have identified in the long process of changing my approach to the Mass. This simple model of how change occurs not only helps me understand how my vision of the Eucharist has shifted over the years; it also offers comfort and reassurance when the process of change begins all over in other areas of my life.

If you are asking questions about the Mass, you are someplace in the process of change—whether you identify with my particular experiences or not. It is possible that you have gone through a reevaluation of the importance of the Mass in your life more than once. Fine! You have experienced the process

29

of change and now can more easily identify what stage you are presently in.

There are four steps in this process: (1) a stable pattern; (2) cracks in the pattern; (3) a time of confusion; (4) an emerging new pattern.

My *stable pattern* was the time I had few if any questions about the Mass. I accepted the catechism-class definition of the Mass and I knew that a Catholic was expected to attend Mass every Sunday. At this stage a person has a pretty firm sense of what to believe and to do.

Cracks appear: In my case, the disillusionment following Vatican Council II and my illness shattered my stable pattern. I began to question what I was doing and why I was doing it. These cracks in our stable structure of thought and practice may appear suddenly in the wake of a crisis or may come slowly and gradually. In any case, they are a turning point.

The cracks introduce a *time of confusion*. I felt confusion most critically while I was living in the seminary without the ordinary duties of parish life. Nothing made much sense to me and I was not sure which way I should go. When one pattern crumbles there is a period of doubt, confusion and turmoil before a new one emerges.

There are three ways we can react at this time. First, we can try to go back to the "good old days" when things were stable and secure—try to put the toothpaste back into the tube. This way leads to stagnation, fossilization of thought and action.

The second way is to opt out of the turmoil and confusion: We can refuse to deal with the crisis and chuck everything because we can't see any easy solution. This way also stifles growth. There is no way to grow without struggle.

The third way is to hang on, to take one tentative step after another. It requires willingness to make mistakes and go up blind alleys, to grope for the light even though we seem to be living in a dense, impenetrable fog. This way can also lead to despair or stagnation, but it is the only possible way to something new and different, vibrant and alive.

Finally, a *new pattern* of stability begins to emerge. In my case I have gradually come to new insights and a different way of thinking about the Mass. The way still is not perfectly clear, but it is clearer than it has been. Some things I thought to be very important about the Mass are no longer important to me.

Other aspects which I seldom considered have become more important.

I have been convinced of the necessity of hanging on, asking questions and reflecting on my experiences. I am convinced that if, with faith and trust, we embrace the search to find personal meaning in the Mass, the time of confusion, futility and doubt will gradually evaporate, and new and deeper relevance will emerge.

The great mystic St. Teresa of Avila struggled with this process for 18 years. She said that for all those years she dreaded going to chapel for prayer and meditation. But in time came those great mystical experiences which meant so much to her and to all those who have read and followed her way.

For Reflection and Sharing

1) Write a brief outline of your reasons and feelings about going to Mass over the years. (Writing forces us to be clear, concise and orderly.)

2) At some time in your life you may have experienced a real change in the way you felt about the Mass or your participation in it. You may have gone more frequently or you may have stopped going; you may have felt more fervor or less; you may have felt that you understood it or you may have discovered that none of it made sense to you. Look at the shift in light of the process of change outlined in the text.

a) Describe how you thought, felt and acted at the time you had a stable pattern of thinking about the Mass and participating in it.

b) What caused the cracks in this stable pattern?

c) Describe how you felt and acted during the unsettling time of confusion which followed the breakdown of the stable pattern.

d) If a new pattern has evolved, describe what it is and how you feel and think about the Mass now.

PART TWO

Exploring Reasons
for Attendance

CHAPTER FOUR

'Many Rooms in My Father's House': The Range of Motives

When I stood at the springs whose waters flow in tiny rivulets into Lake Itasca in northwestern Minnesota, it was difficult for me to picture a river 2,500 miles long, in places half a mile wide and deep enough to swallow a 10-story building. But the mighty Mississippi has its beginnings in the gentle trickle of water from those springs.

If Lake Itasca alone fed the Father of Waters it would be no more than a small river just like thousands of others in the Land of 10,000 Lakes. But the Ohio, the Missouri, the Red and the Arkansas as well as 36 other navigable rivers and 200 smaller streams feed the Mississippi on its long journey to the sea. If Lake Itasca dried up, even if a river such as the Illinois ceased to flow, it would make little difference to the Mississippi. It would continue to roll on, fed by other tributaries. But if *all* the major tributaries were diverted, the Mississippi would become a small, lazy stream meandering through the heart of our nation.

Most people who go to church on Sunday are carried there by a conviction that has been fed from many sources. If they had but one reason, one motive, and that motive dried up, they could easily spend Sunday morning in bed, on the tennis court or at the beach. But if people's reasons for celebrating the Eucharist are many and varied, they will always have enough energy to participate even though this or that reason may no longer make much sense to them. I wonder how much the decline in Sunday Mass attendance is due to the fact that many Catholics only have a single motive: fear of hell. Once they no longer feel it is a sin to miss Mass on Sunday, they stop attending, at least regularly.

Since beginning this book I have asked many people why they go to Mass. Their answers (motives) have varied greatly. A group of seven priests gave five different answers, none of which matched those given by a group of seven laywomen. (Incidentally, each of the priests vehemently defended his position as *the* reason the celebration of the Eucharist is meaningful and important.)

Answers I have heard cover a wide range of motives:

"It is a time to visit my Father and I feel good being there."

"I go to Mass to acknowledge the presence of the Lord in my life and to show him that I love him."

"We come together to publicly acknowledge the Lord."

"I find peace there—especially after I have had a fight with one of the kids and he slips into the pew next to me."

"I get the strength I need to face my daily problems."

"I choose to go because it is a privilege."

"I go every Sunday to check in and check up on myself. If I didn't do that weekly I would soon begin to slip away from my faith."

"I experience a change of heart when I need it."

"It is a time to pray to God."

"It is an effective way to ask God for the things I need."

"At the Eucharist I celebrate what has been happening in the community."

"It is a time when I sit at the Last Supper table with Jesus and his apostles."

"I go to receive Communion. That's what counts."

"I go to be inspired and encouraged by the words of the priest."

Any Motive Is Good

In my search for reasons why people go to Mass, I turned to the Scriptures to see whether the stories of the many meals Jesus had with people would offer a clue. It seems rather obvious that Martha and Mary had him to dinner because they loved him and were his close friends. Levi and Zacchaeus put on banquets for him because they were grateful that he had accepted them into the company of his followers. They were financially well-off but social outcasts, men barred from the synagogue because they served the Romans as tax collectors.

It is a bit harder to figure out why the Pharisees invited Jesus, but he seems to have dined with them frequently. In one case it is obvious that the invitation was a trap: A leader of the Pharisees had him to dinner in order to catch him saying or doing something contrary to the Law. In another case the motive is harder to discern—the host was so ungracious as to neglect to wash Jesus' feet or to anoint his head with oil.

The one thing evident in the Scripture stories is that Jesus was not too concerned *why* people invited him to dinner. Whatever their motives, he used the occasion to try to bring them a little closer to the Kingdom. Jesus welcomed people who were sinners, outcasts, aliens. The stories show that the Eucharist is a time of forgiveness, of sharing what we have with others, of giving thanks, of welcoming all into our community.

The Gospels force me to conclude that practically any motive for coming to Mass is good. If our motives are not as pure and noble as those of the mystics and saints, we have to be patient with ourselves because God has not yet finished with us. Because we are still rough and unpolished, our motives need not be of the highest order.

I like the attitude of the monsignor who, every Easter and Christmas, welcomes those who do not come to church regularly. (He does not do this in the condemnatory and cynical spirit in which I once wished people a Merry Christmas on Easter Sunday because I would not see them again until the next Easter.) In a warm, kindly way he tells them he is happy to see them whenever and for whatever reason they come.

Why People Don't Go to Mass

Over the years I have heard many reasons why people have given up going to Mass. They blame the priest who was inconsiderate when Grandmother died. They conclude that Mass attendance does no good because the people they see in church pray to God on Sunday and prey on their neighbors on Monday. They cite distance, the petty rivalries in the women's group, lack of appropriate clothes or any one of a million excuses. I have never found a convincing response to their reasoning.

But there is one excuse for which I feel there is a powerful and appropriate response. When people say that they do not attend Mass because they feel guilty or unworthy, I try to help them see that Jesus was talking precisely about them and to them when he said, "The healthy do not need a doctor; sick people do. I have not come to invite the self-righteous to a change of heart, but sinners" (Luke 5:31-32). I tell them the story of the woman whose sins were forgiven because she loved much (Luke 7:36-50) and of the man who was healed because he trusted (Luke 10:46-52).

One thing I do know: Participating at Mass is not the reward for being good. Mass is the place we hear the call to give up our sin and to learn to love more completely. Perhaps, in the last analysis, one of the best reasons for going to Mass is a realization that we are weak, that we are sinners, that we have failed and will fail again—and that the greatest sign of our love and trust is that we keep coming back to the Lord even when we have lost faith in ourselves.

In the next few chapters we will take a closer look at five categories of reasons for going to Mass. I am sure that you will think of other ones, perhaps better ones. But before we move on, take some time to identify the reasons *you* now have for going to church on Sunday.

For Reflection and Sharing

1) Read one or two of the meal stories in the Gospel of Luke and put yourself in the place of the host or hostess. What reasons would you have for inviting Jesus to dinner if you were:
—Martha (Luke 10:38-42)?

—Levi (Luke 5:27-32)?

—Zacchaeus (Luke 19:1-10)?

—a Pharisee (Luke 7:36-50; 11:37-54; 14:1-24)?

2) What are the reasons you now have for going to Mass on Sunday? How do your reasons compare with those of the people whose stories you just read?

3) What are some reasons your friends give for going to Mass?

4) Which of their reasons give you food for thought when you are reflecting on your own motives?

CHAPTER FIVE

'Thou Shalt':
Mass as an Obligation

It is always a revelation for me
to stay for a few days in a home in which there are young
children. Time after time I have seen parents reach total
frustration trying to explain to a child *why* he or she should eat
what was on the plate, go to bed, or turn off the TV. Reasons
bounce off the child without making the slightest impression
until the parents fall back on the oldest reason of all: "Because
I said so!"

When we grow up we continue to ask *why*. Often the
reasons given fail to impress us because they do not resonate
with our experience, our feelings, our ideas. Likewise, when
people ask *why* they should go to Mass, the reasons given in
the liturgical documents and in sermons seem to make little or
no impression on them. For many people God's "because I said
so" (the Third Commandment) is still the strongest motive.

It would be an ideal world if all people based their
decisions and actions on the highest interior principle: justice
based on love. But modern developmental psychologists have
found that relatively few people base their decisions on noble
principles. Even those who sometimes do so also make choices
based on lesser motives at different times and in different
circumstances.

What are some of the other motives people have for
acting? One is fear—a powerful and effective way to make us
do things for our own good. Every time I see a black and white
California Highway Patrol car sitting on the shoulder of the

41

freeway, I slow down to 55. It is fear of a ticket and the consequent fine rather than respect for a reasonable law which prompts me to drive at a safer speed. If we had absolutely no fear of anything, few if any of us would live to puberty.

Another powerful motive is hope for a reward. This reward may be physical (such as the candy we promise a child for being good), or it may be psychological (the approval of parents or peers). It may even be the reward of self-approval, the feeling that we have achieved our goals or lived up to our standards.

Fear of punishment and hope for reward were the underlying reasons many preachers formerly gave for regular attendance at Mass. They painted in lurid detail the physical torments which awaited those who neglected Sunday Mass without reason. They also held out the promise of a reward to those who attended regularly—namely, an easy and happy life in heaven and material help from God in time of need on this earth. To be sure, most priests also preached about the meaning of the Mass and gave many other reasons why people should attend. But I am always amazed at how few people heard those reasons and how many heard the threats.

I question whether a rip-roaring sermon on the hell-fire awaiting those who deliberately miss on Mass on Sunday would be very effective today. Too many people do not take the existence of hell seriously. Even those who do have a difficult time reconciling the idea of a good, loving, forgiving God with such extreme punishment. The fact that one distances oneself from a loving Father by consistently and without reason missing Mass on Sunday does not seem to make an impression on people.

Another reason why the old-fashioned mission sermon has so little impact today is that Catholics are beginning to take more and more responsibility for making their own choices and deciding what is right or wrong in particular cases. Church laws and regulations are not taken as seriously as they once were.

Community Ties

If the fear of hell is not the motive it once was, other forms of reward and punishment still stir people to action. For instance, we all have a deep desire to feel that we belong to some group or other. Very few people are total loners who want to identify with no one, no group. The price for membership in a group (a family, a team, a club, a clan) is usually conformity to the norms of that group. The reward for that conformity is acceptance; the punishment for nonconformity may be exclusion.

The need to belong is a powerful motive—for evil as well as for good. I recently met a 15-year-old boy convicted of murder. Told to shoot another teenager, a member of a different gang, he had killed to protect his standing in his own gang.

On the positive side, I once visited a small Swiss village where everyone was in church every Sunday. I had just come from an Italian town where 90 percent of the men waited at the local tavern while their wives and children went to Mass. Curious about the difference, I asked the Swiss pastor how he managed to get the men to come. His answer was simple: "We are a small community, all Catholic. We know each other. If someone is not sick and misses Mass, his neighbors want to know why."

The desire to identify with a group is natural and surely has motivated many Catholics to be faithful. They see regular Mass attendance as a sign of their Catholic identity. Perhaps this motive is not the highest, but it is very helpful. It helps people recognize, accept and value practices which the community of believing Catholics has found help nourish their relationship to God and to one another.

Another related motive is respect for the law. A more refined motive than concern about reward and punishment, it looks beyond the individual's preferences to more general norms which apply to all people.

The purpose of law is to help people achieve some end. In civil society it ensures order and peace so that we can pursue life, liberty and happiness. Church laws not only achieve order in the community but also help each individual grow spiritually. They are intended to help us enrich and deepen our relationship with God and with one another. Those laws which pertain most directly to the lives of all the faithful have grown out of the accumulated wisdom of the centuries. They embody certain essential things people need to do, at least in a minimal way, in order to be faithful to the gospel.

One such law is Canon 1274: "On Sundays and holy days of obligation, the faithful are obliged to assist at Mass." At one time in the history of the Church there was no such law. It was

43

only when Christians grew lax in their participation in the Eucharist and drifted away from living according to gospel values that the Church felt the need for legislation. Gradually, insightful Christians realized that to live the Christian life fully and fruitfully one should share in the Lord's Last Supper on a regular weekly basis. (Of course, mere observance of the law without an accompanying interior conviction will not produce more growth in one's relationship to God and to neighbor.)

Church law does not have the same impact on people as it did 35 years ago. Attending Mass out of a sense of obligation has gone out of fashion. But as a motive, it is not all bad. People who are so motivated should be reassured that they have not completely missed the boat. If nothing else, observance of the law leads to the development of a habit.

The Force of Habit

Habits guide 99 percent of our daily actions. If we had to examine the many options open to us just from the time we get up in the morning to the time we leave for work, we would seldom get out of the house before noon. We would have to consider the pros and cons of getting out of bed, the reasons for cleaning our teeth and washing up, the value of wearing clothes versus going naked, and why we should wear modern American styles rather than toga or kilt, sari or sarong. By the time we finally arrived at our place of work, we would be in a state of complete mental exhaustion.

Habit makes ordinary decisions easy and conserves energy for the new and trying things which come up each day. Church law can help us develop the good habit of setting aside a certain time for God and the community every Sunday.

Dependence on habits generated by the law carries some risks, of course. A person may confuse the *means* (presence at the Eucharist) with the *end* (union with God and the Christian community). It can also lead to hypocrisy when a person's life does not match what his or her action professes on Sunday morning.

Our desire to keep the law can even keep us from reflecting on our own personal motives and embracing more important motives for coming to the table of the Lord. If we have to go, no questions asked, then we may feel that there is no need to examine the reasons for joining the community in celebrating the Eucharist. Finally, habit formed by law can become robot-like and cause us to perform the action mechanically, without any thought of what we actually are doing.

But, ideally, law should free us to ask why weekly Mass is considered so important by the community. Then real personal conviction can rise from reflecting on our experiences, from prayer, from examining our other motives and the reasons the community has for the practice.

Damaging Attitudes

Certain subtle attitudes prevalent in our society militate powerfully against seeing the reasonableness and importance of the Sunday obligation. I hesitate to mention these because each of them is grounded in a good and legitimate human need. It is not the need itself that causes a problem, but the attitude people develop to *meet* it.

We all have a real and legitimate need to enjoy life in the here-and-now, to make sense out of our world and out of what we are doing. But this need can generate a demand for instant satisfaction and obvious relevance in the here-and-now from everything we do. This attitude is the problem.

Experience teaches us that it is often necessary to put off immediate gratification for some future and better good. It also teaches that things which give instant and momentary satisfaction may not always be the best for us in the long run. (The use of drugs is a prime example.) Experience also teaches that it is unreasonable to reject something just because we do not immediately see its value. Often enough it takes time for us to discover the gold buried in practices which do not appeal to us at a particular time. The craving for instant satisfaction, however, can cause people to leave the tutelage of the law long before they have gained enough experience to see for themselves the value of the Mass.

Another very fundamental human need is for the freedom to make personal choices. But freedom carries with it a very heavy responsibility to examine seriously the options open, to consider the consequences and, finally, to weigh options not only in the light of our own desires but also in the light of the accumulated wisdom of the community and of our ultimate destiny.

A person is free, of course, to make a decision without due consideration and to make a decision which will later have disastrous consequences. One of the purposes of the law of Sunday observance is to protect people from themselves when they do not or cannot weigh options and consequences.

A third legitimate need is to develop our own individual talents and to do things in the best way *we* can do them. Yet this need can generate an attitude which claims that what we *feel* like doing is the determining factor in all decisions. Thus a person who does not like going to Mass feels that it is right not to go. People with this attitude may excuse themselves by saying that they can pray better on the beach, in the mountains, in the quiet of their room.

No doubt at certain times we all can pray better when we are alone. But the accumulated experience of the People of God is that most people will not go to the beach or to the mountains on a regular basis. Plus, we are not isolated individuals, each taking his or her own private path to God. We are baptized into a community. We live and die in that community, and in that community together we worship the Lord. The Church law protects us from the extreme individualism which recognizes only our own thoughts and feelings as a guide on the journey through life.

Foundation for Growth

All the motives we have are good, even the motive of fear of hell. Any of them serves us well at one time or another. Each puts us into a different relationship with God and with our fellow Christians; each has some power to move us. But as we grow our motives must change. What was sufficient when we were children is inadequate when we are adults.

All the reasons for Mass attendance which flow from a sense of obligation, which respond to a "Thou shalt" out of fear or respect, need to be examined by adults called to the freedom of God's children. Fear of punishment and respect for law *can* provide a basis for further growth. But this growth depends on an inner conviction that the purpose of the Church's law concerning Mass on Sunday is to help us do what we are called to do by Baptism and to stimulate us to look more deeply into the meaning of the Eucharist for our daily life.

For Reflection and Sharing

Before you proceed further in looking at your motives for going to Mass, reflect upon your experiences with rules, regulations and laws to see what *good* impact they have had on you.

1) List three or four good habits or practices which you feel contribute to the quality of your life, but which came from rules and regulations your parents imposed upon you as a child.

2) Reflect on how you came to see the value of those habits:
   a) How did you feel about those rules when you were a child? Did you grasp the importance of the underlying reasons?

   b) What caused your understanding of the reasons behind those rules to change?

   c) How do you feel about those rules and regulations now, and how do you feel about your present habits?

3) Has the Church law of Mass on Sunday helped you develop your habit of going to Mass and improve your relationship to God?

4) How powerful at the present time is your sense of obligation rising from the Church law to attend Mass on Sunday?

5) What would you say to someone who says that his or her *only* reason for going to Mass is fear of hell or compliance with Church law?

CHAPTER SIX

'The Better Part':
Looking for Inspiration

More and more people are
consciously saying, "I *want* to go to Mass," rather than, "I gotta
go." Their reasons for saying this are many and varied, but one
theme frequently emerges: "I go on Sunday for a bit of
encouragement or inspiration"; "I need help with living"; "I
want to learn how to cope with life better."

Most likely it was this kind of yearning that moved Mary
to the feet of Jesus while Martha slaved in the kitchen (Luke
10:38-42). It certainly was the reason why the two disciples began
to talk with the stranger on the road to Emmaus (Luke 24:13-35).

I like to imagine that during the Liturgy of the Word we
are doing the same thing Mary and those two disciples did. They
talked with Jesus about life and, in the process, their lives became
better and a bit easier.

I picture Jesus sitting cross-legged on the floor in the home
of Mary and Martha, leaning back against a wall with a cup of
wine or cool water in his hand, unwinding after a hard day
spent tramping from village to village. I see Mary sitting nearby,
looking at him with love and concern. She is asking how the
day went, what new questions the disciples brought up, whom
Jesus cured and, especially, what he told the people. I hear Jesus
talking about the farmers, the birds of the air, the lazy son, the
prodigal son. Mary drinks it all in. She is getting to know how
this man whom she loves thinks and feels and sees life.

Then, suddenly, I hear Martha's shrill voice demanding
that Mary get busy. And I hear Jesus' gentle rebuke that Mary

has chosen the better part.

Some Scripture commentators think that St. Luke put Martha in the story as an object lesson to people in his community who were too concerned about the way their homes looked when Christians gathered for the Eucharist. At times I wish that liturgy committees would read this story before planning for a big celebration. The first thing I would like them to consider is how they might enhance the words of Scripture so that the people would drink them in as Mary drank in the words of Jesus. I get upset when special music has been practiced, the church decorated, banners hung—but no one has bothered either to ask the preacher what he is going to talk about or to suggest a theme he might follow. At times I feel that Martha has finally managed to get Mary on her feet while Jesus talks to himself.

I also wish that homilists would make encouragement and hope the foundation of all their talks. People have a hard enough time with life during the week. Things go wrong. Their self-image takes a few blows. They may have failed miserably. They don't need to be put down in church, to be scolded for their faults every Sunday. On the other hand, they need more than a Pollyanna approach to life. They need compassion and understanding for their weaknesses, reassurance that God still loves them and hope that they will be able to do a bit better.

The Homily—The 'Better Part'?

I realize that in many cases the homily isn't worth listening to. I know that most of the time when I sit in the pews I am bored or angry with what I hear. Some priests just do not have the vitality and the skills to preach well. Others never seem to have a new idea or to see how the Scriptures relate to the real world.

In times past I blamed poor homilies on our lack of training. For many centuries preaching at Mass was not a high priority. When I was in the seminary we studied moral theology for four years so we could hear confessions well; we studied Scripture and other branches of theology. But we had no classes on how to communicate what we learned to the people except a one-semester class in preaching. In six years in the seminary I preached one practice sermon and, if I remember accurately,

I had to write five sample sermons.

A classmate of mine expressed the prevailing attitude perfectly to an elderly lady he met on a train. When she found out that he was a Catholic priest, she asked: "Why are Catholic priests such poor preachers? I am not Catholic, but I do go to Catholic services at times, and I find that your sermons are consistently poorer than those I hear in Protestant churches."

John had the answer on the tip of his tongue: "We are a sacramental Church. The most important thing for us is the celebration of the Eucharist and the sacraments. We are not like Protestant ministers, who are primarily preachers."

Thank heavens this attitude is now dead, but its effects still linger on. Priests still do not make the time to prepare well, or to read materials other than theological books. Yet some of the most effective sermons I have heard sprang from books of psychology, sociology or business management. The preacher had read something about what the people in the pews experience and saw how the Scriptures expressed the same reality in a different idiom.

I marvel at the way people cope with dry, dull, dreary sermons. A Sister I know tells of going to Mass with her Aunt Jane. The homily was terrible. The priest rambled on and on, covering the Creed and all Ten Commandments, with a dose of the sacraments thrown in for good measure. When they left church, the nun exploded and sounded off for five minutes. Aunt Jane said sweetly, "But, dear, you *listened* to him!"

"Didn't you?" the Sister asked.

"Of course not. I never do. He is like that all the time," replied the aunt.

"Then what did you do during the sermon?" the Sister asked.

"What I always do. I planned my menus for the week and made up my shopping list in my head. Then I went over my upcoming engagements, and by the time I had my week all worked out, he was finished."

In contrast, the disciples on the road to Emmaus were so taken with Jesus' explanation of the Scriptures that their doubts were resolved, their discouragement overcome and their spirits raised. They were so engrossed in his words that they lost track of time; it was evening when they reached the end of their journey. They begged the stranger to stay. When he broke bread with them, they recognized him. If the homilies we hear today could captivate and encourage people as Jesus' words captivated those two discouraged disciples, all of us—priests and laity—would much more readily recognize Jesus in the breaking of the bread and in our daily lives.

So when I preach, I watch for the people who try to escape my words with the same technique I used when a noted cardinal preached. For years he gave his very erudite sermons; for years I went to sleep exactly 122 seconds after he began. When I see someone's head begin to nod, I know it is time to quit or to switch gears completely.

There are ways priests can improve their homilies. They are nothing new; they are in all the books on preaching—study, preparation, consultation with confreres, posture and voice control, simplicity, etc. But what can laypeople do to help priests inspire them, help them live more fulfilling lives and get to know Jesus better?

Beyond Patient Suffering

For one thing, they can *compliment* a preacher when he *has* made a point which touched their lives. I appreciate it and try harder when a person comes up and says, "I really heard what you said about affirming my kids. I'll try it."

Laypeople can also *let priests know* what problems and life situations they would like to hear him address. This kind of sharing is becoming more open as parishes form more and more small groups. I have just sat in on three different groups and listened to divorced people talk about their pain. I know that a great deal of what I heard will work its way into my sermons on family life. I will be speaking from real situations rather than from some textbook theory.

In the long run, however, laypeople cannot expect the priest to do all the work. Neither can they expect every priest to be another Fulton Sheen. They have to take some responsibility themselves. There is something *you* can do to make the readings and the homily more fruitful in your life: *prepare.*

The day before (not just five minutes before) Mass, read the three Scripture selections and ask what they mean in your life. At first the applications which you have heard a dozen times will come to your mind. But try to see something new.

Pick one little section of the Gospel and use your imagination to re-create the scene as I did earlier with Mary sitting at Jesus' feet. Imagine the dialogue between the people in the story. Place yourself in the scene as an observer: What do you see, hear, smell, feel and think? When you read the Epistle pretend you are hearing one side of a telephone conversation and try to guess what the person at the other end is saying.

You may even want to turn to commentaries to get a bit more information. These may be helpful, especially those which try to relate the Bible to life. Just a few minutes reflecting on the readings by yourself will put you into a very receptive frame of mind when the lectors read the Scriptures and the priest or deacon gives the homily.

Not being a family man, I am not sure whether my last suggestion has any merit. It may be just another one of those good ideas that are not practical. But isn't it possible for family members gathered for Saturday supper to read aloud the Scriptures for the next day and to spend a few minutes talking about what the readings say to each of them?

I was surprised when one elderly woman said that she had never heard a sermon without getting something from it. The more I think about it the more I admire her attitude. She was not expecting much, but she realized that she could get something out of any homily if she listened for the few words or phrases which spoke to her.

The Spirit of God does not transform poorly prepared homilies into pearls of wisdom or infuse life into a dead delivery. On the other hand, even God cannot get through to a critical listener who is setting impossible standards for an inspiring homily.

For Reflection and Sharing

1) What do you usually get out of the homilies you hear in your parish church? Why?

2) What practical way could you better prepare yourself to listen to the readings and the homily?

3) What was the most inspiring sermon you have heard? Why did it touch you?

4) Have you ever sincerely complimented a priest on his homily or kindly suggested a way of improving it a bit? What happened when you did?

CHAPTER SEVEN

'Ask and Receive':
The Mass and Our Needs

I once thought it was silly to
ask God for help. After all, he knows everything. In Scripture,
Jesus says that the Father knows what I need even before I ask
and that he keeps track of the few hairs left on my head. Yet,
interestingly enough, Jesus did not tell us *not* to ask. He just
said to keep our prayer short and to the point. But, at any rate,
asking for help was not a very strong motive impelling me to
participate in the Eucharist.

But then I had a change of heart. One day a co-worker,
Sister Mary Michael, O.P., convinced me during a very casual
conversation that asking God's help is good and necessary. The
reason we ask, she said, was not to bring our needs to *God's*
attention, but to focus *our* attention on our limitations, our
powerlessness, our need for God's help. Maybe you already
know this (St. Augustine said the same thing 16 centuries ago),
but I am a slow learner. It took me a long time to discover the
real value of prayers of petition.

Today I bring my list of petitions to every Mass. The level
of the trust and faith with which I make these petitions varies
greatly, I must admit. It is rather weak when I pray for the cure
of a friend who has terminal cancer, or the end of the nuclear
arms race, or the conversion of Russia. These requests can only
be answered by a miracle of the first magnitude—and I don't
expect many such miracles to occur in my life.

My feelings are reflected in the experience of a
priest-friend who was being hounded to enshrine a certain statue

55

of Our Lady in the church and to begin a novena for the conversion of Russia. He refused. He pointed out that billions of Hail Mary's for the conversion of Russia had already been said in the years after World War I with little effect. He could see no reason to add another novena. He suggested instead that people begin to pray that their own hearts be changed. Then they could love the Communists as brothers and sisters rather than see them as the cause of all the mischief in the world.

My faith and trust level is much higher when I ask for help in situations over which I have a great deal of control. Then I can ask for knowledge to see the situation clearly, for wisdom to make the right choices, for courage to put those choices into practice in the face of the fear which often grips my heart and, finally and most importantly, I can ask for the ability to grasp what God wants me to learn from the situation.

In situations where I have little or no control I simply pray: "God, you can bring marvelous things out of the most difficult and messy circumstances. What I can't do I leave up to you." I have seen too many signs of God's concern for me not to trust in the most difficult personal situations. As someone once put it, a sign from God is simply a coincidence seen through the eyes of faith.

For example, I prayed for years for relief from stomach trouble. One day a priest dropped in the rectory, the first and only time he visited me. Seeing my distress, he suggested that I see a therapist. I said *he* was crazy, not me! Six months later, when I was willing to talk to the devil if it would help me feel better, I took his advice. In therapy I realized that my stomach problems came in great part from the pressures of my living situation. When I found a way to change that, I began to feel better. Was the priest's visit merely a coincidence, or was it a sign of God's concern for me? Whatever it was, it convinced me that God works in wonderful and strange ways in my life, that prayers for help are effective, and that "asking" at Mass is a most effective way to get the help I need.

Attitudes for the Table

All the cures in the New Testament attest to the fact that Jesus does answer our requests for help. St. Luke places one of these cures at a dinner given by a leader of the Pharisees (Luke

14:1-27). One of the guests had dropsy. He was sick and needed help. The account does not mention that he asked for a cure; evidently Jesus read an unspoken plea in the man's heart. First he put the rigoristic interpreters of the Law on the defensive by asking them if it was lawful to cure on the Sabbath. When they remained silent, he answered his own question by curing the man and sending him on his way.

From this story it is obvious that when we come to the Lord's table we can ask for what we need. But St. Luke's inclusion of Jesus' words to the assembled guests stresses that we must also come with certain attitudes.

Jesus rebuked those who were vying for the best places at table. He said the first would be last and the last first. In other words, people who come to the table of the Lord must approach it with *humility*.

In St. Luke's community some Christians felt that, because of their power, wealth or prestige, they deserved the best places at the table when the Eucharist was celebrated. Twentieth-century believers do not jockey to sit in the first pew or on the altar as princes and nobles did in ages gone by, but our hearts may still be filled with self-righteousness and hardened with a rigorism which lays heavy burdens on those around us.

Jesus also told his host not to invite his friends and those capable of repaying him to a banquet, but rather the poor, the lame, the outcasts who could never repay. In other words, the attitude of people who want to sit at table with Jesus must be one of *generosity* with no thought of reward.

Finally, Jesus spoke of the people who refused to come to the king's banquet. (He was speaking of the Messianic banquet of which our table-sharing is a foretaste.) Those who refuse to come are those who reject the demands of humility, who set their own rules to govern God's goodness and who are not willing to share with the poor without expectation of reward.

The human tendencies which interfere with God's call to salvation were evident to Jesus in those people who felt salvation lay in the Law, not in their heart. They were evident to St. Luke in the community for which he wrote his Gospel. And, sad to say, I find evidence of these same tendencies in my own heart when I sit with my community at daily Mass.

Our Need for Forgiveness

Our failure to express adequately these attitudes which Jesus requires for his table fellowship remind us of a need we all have: the need for forgiveness.

In days gone by Catholics were most careful to bring their grocery list of habitual faults to confession every week (or at least once a month). Each Saturday I left the confessional feeling as if I had been pelted to death with popcorn: The people on the other side of the grille had missed their morning prayers, been angry with the children, used bad words and said unkind things. I felt the time was mostly wasted because I seldom heard from a sinner truly sorry for a life spent away from God. Now that I sit face-to-face with penitents and talk about their life, their sense of guilt, their efforts to grow, I really enjoy hearing confessions.

In the past people did not really believe that venial sins were forgiven by good acts and, especially, by the Penitential Rite of the Mass. Therefore they confessed *everything* to the priest. Today the pendulum has swung the other way. Many Catholics feel that confession is no longer necessary and that the "Lord, have mercy" suffices in all circumstances for reconciliation with God and with the Church.

Ah, well, that's the human condition. But in that beautiful story of the sinful woman who washed Jesus' feet (Luke 7:36-50), we discover that the Eucharist *is* a time of forgiveness, of reconciliation, of welcoming sinners back into the fold.

In this story Simon, an important Pharisee, invited Jesus to dinner, but neglected to show him the common courtesy of washing his feet and anointing his head with oil. A woman from the city, a well-known sinner (most likely the local prostitute), walked in unannounced, fell at the feet of Jesus, washed his feet with her tears, wiped them with her hair and anointed them with very expensive perfume. After rebuking Simon, Jesus simply said that "her many sins are forgiven...because of her great love."

Love—for Jesus and for all his brothers and sisters, shown by whatever means we feel appropriate—and sorrow for the past are the two essential attitudes we need if our request for forgiveness is to be effective. Change of behavior and of life-style will flow from these attitudes.

Food for the Needy

I go to the table of the Lord because I am needy. I need forgiveness for my sins and for all the dumb things I do. I need help in my daily work, in writing this manuscript, in relating to the people around me. The more conscious of my needs I become, the more often and the more fervently I celebrate the Eucharist.

And that's true of all of us. I have known people who, when they were in dire need, would come to Mass daily. But they would soon slide back into their old habits when that need was met. I have also met people who are so conscious of their dependence on God that it takes a very serious reason to keep them away from *daily* Mass.

For Reflection and Sharing

1) How is the frequency and fervor of your attendance at Mass affected by the depth of your need?

2) What are some of the things you pray for at Mass? With what degree of fervor and belief do you pray for each of them?

3) The Eucharist is a time of reconciliation not only with God but with one another. Jesus advises: "If you bring your gift to the altar and there recall that your brother has anything against you, leave your gift at the altar, and go first to be reconciled with your brother, and then come and offer your gift" (Matthew 5:23-24). These words apply especially to our relations with the people closest to us—spouses, children, close friends.

    a) Is the Mass a time the family is usually reconciled and at peace? Why or why not?

    b) What instances can you recall when you or some member of your family followed Jesus' advice?

CHAPTER EIGHT

'Given for You':
The Mass as an Expression of Love

The reasons we have for going to Mass remind me of an artichoke. This rather ugly, cone-shaped relative of the thistle has layer upon layer of tightly packed leaves. Only a tiny section at the base of each leaf is edible. One has to peel one layer of leaves after another to get to the large, soft, delicious heart of the artichoke.

Similarly, we have to peel away one by one the motives we have for going to Mass until we get to the ultimate reason—which can only be love. Every other motive is good—but inadequate.

The Mass is more than a time spent in church because the law requires it. It is more than an opportunity to enjoy an inspiring homily and uplifting songs. It is more than a time to ask God for the things we need, or a time to pray quietly. All these reasons for being at Mass are good, but they are like the outer leaves of the artichoke.

We are closer to the heart of the Mass when we come together to share table fellowship in memory of Christ. Fellowship implies concern for one another, love for one another. Celebrating in memory of Christ implies that it is love for God which brings us together.

That word *love*, however, causes me a great deal of difficulty. It connotes feelings of affection and warmth, and I have to admit that I practically never feel warm and affectionate about God. I have read about saints who were so wrapped up in loving communion with God that they lost all sense of time and place at Mass. But I am always conscious of time and place; no great emotions sweep over me at the Consecration or Communion.

I constantly ask myself whether my relationship with God is really one of love. And when I read the Gospels and see how Jesus showed his love for his Father by preaching and caring for people, how much time he spent in prayer, how faithful he was to his other duties as a Jew, I often wonder whether I love God at all.

I have read many books on the nature of love. I have little trouble seeing how what they say describes God's love for me but, for the life of me, I cannot grasp what they say about my love for God. Jesuit Father John Powell says that we love when the well-being, the security and the happiness of another is as important to us as our own well-being, security and happiness. I know from Scripture that God has just such a love for me. But how can I lessen or increase God's happiness, security or well-being? He can take care of these matters much better than I.

In his book *Man's Search for Meaning*, Victor Frankl defines the essence of love as bringing out the good which another does not even realize he or she possesses. My life is witness to the fact that God is constantly trying to do that for me. Imagine the consummate pride of thinking a person can do that for God!

H. Scott Peck, author of *The Road Less Traveled*, identifies love with "the will to extend one's self for the purpose of nurturing one's own or another's spiritual growth." I can see how God nurtures my growth, but I haven't the slightest idea of what I can do to nurture his.

I know that all these writers have in some way glimpsed love's mystery. But I still have to put together a patchwork of ideas to try to express for myself the meaning of "the love of God" in my life.

For me the words of the Our Father describe my understanding of love for God better than any definition of love. I try in my own flawed, cockeyed way to praise (to "hallow") God's name—and to draw others into praise. I do my best to help his "Kingdom come"—into my heart and into the hearts of others. This Kingdom is simply the desire to do the Father's will, to share with others freely, to forgive others unconditionally and to bear the pain and suffering which come from these efforts. I trust that God will daily feed and care for me, forgive me and, most of all, "deliver me from evil"—keep me from straying too far from him.

I try not to rattle through the Our Father as I used to do. I have to be pretty muddleheaded not to put some feeling into that prayer no matter how poorly I may say the other prayers at Mass.

What does this seeming digression on the nature of love have to do with going to Mass? Simply this: Love has to be manifested in words and deeds. It cannot be kept locked up in the heart. When we go to Mass we have to realize that we are serving that very human need to *express* love.

God does not need our love. *We* need to express it in word and action or it will die. God does not need our prayers; he already knows all. *We* need to bring into consciousness our needs and dispositions. God does not need ritual. But *we* need to express our deepest desires and feelings in actions as well as in words. God gets nothing from what we do. But *we* get everything from our worship when it brings us into closer union with God and opens us to receive his blessings.

Love Means Sacrifice

There is still another level of meaning, one which is the very heart of the Eucharist. Without it the Mass would be no different than any other prayer service, any other gathering of friends and neighbors. This level of meaning was expressed in the past by the phrase "the Holy Sacrifice of the Mass."

The connotations of the word *sacrifice*—death, blood, innocent victim, suffering, cruelty—for many years blocked my appreciation of the reality of the love it implies. We live light-years of custom and thought away from the time when our ancestors offered oxen and grain to God. We cannot easily grasp the idea that through offering these gifts people were seeking to unite themselves with God. But giving to God a portion of the crops and animals on which their very survival depended represented the surrender of their whole life, their whole being, to God. And God, by accepting their gifts, bound himself to them in a special way.

In some way which we do not understand (and which theologians have, without remarkable clarity, tried for centuries to explain), Jesus united us with God by his death and resurrection. When God accepted the gift of Jesus' life, he bound himself to all of us in a *family* relationship; Jesus' sacrifice made us God's daughters and sons, his heirs, sharers in his very life.

By achieving this secure place in God's love for us, Jesus opened new possibilities for us to become loving people—people who love not only God, but ourselves and one another as well. He promised to be with us, to help us keep his commandment to love one another as he has loved us.

By inviting us to do what he did at the Last Supper, Jesus invites us to offer ourselves in love and obedience to the Father. By giving us himself as our spiritual food, Jesus unites us with God, our Father, and gives us the strength we need gradually to become one in love.

Mass, then, is a time we take out of our ordinary routine to *remember* that we are a loved people, a holy people. It is a time to speak our gratitude for God's love. It is an opportunity to express our love and to show it by offering a gift which represents our lives to the Father. In a way difficult for us to comprehend except by faith, we join Christ in offering himself to the Father. But that gift is not *our* real gift of love unless there is something of ourselves in it. Our very presence shows that we want to be part of Christ's sacrifice, but we can be more specific about the gifts we have to offer.

Sometimes I take a few minutes before Mass to prepare four small gifts to offer to the Father as a sign of my love. The first is *a sin or fault* of which I am particularly conscious. This is a strange gift, but a real one. Christ came to take away our sins and I am willing to give him one to take out of my life. It is helpful to acknowledge in a general way during the Penitential Rite that we are sinners, but we have to focus on specific aspects of that sinfulness or we will never make any progress in overcoming our sins and faults.

Next I prepare a small gift to show my trust in my Father. As I say, "Let us pray," at the beginning of Mass, I ask for *something I need*. The prayers of the Roman rite are brief, stark and simple. Many people have complained that these prayers have lost their beauty in the revision of the Mass. I find just the opposite. I can make the Opening Prayer my own because its simple words leave room for my personal needs. They speak of love, forgiveness, unity, life, harmony and peace—words which take on vitality precisely because they echo my own need.

The third gift of love I bring is *something I have done for another*. Since my last Mass I may have shared some of the bounty the Lord has showered on me, or forgiven someone, or tried to promote peace and harmony, or helped someone in pain or in need. This tiny gift I place on the paten as I prepare the gifts of bread and wine and say the offertory prayers.

The final gift is a simple *thank you* for something good that has happened to me. This gift I present when I invite the congregation to join me in the Prayer After Communion.

As I said earlier, I know not what love means when we talk about relationship to God. I only hope the Lord understands that the flawed gifts I offer are the best I can do at this time.

Love Without Faith Is Impossible

In all honesty, I have to admit that love is not always my motive for celebrating the Eucharist. I suspect, however, that a great many people who have given up attending Mass have never seriously grappled with this level of meaning. When I have tried to express it in order to encourage a person to return to the Lord's table, I have usually encountered a blank stare of incomprehension.

I suspect that the kind of love which moves us to see beyond what we hear and feel and see at the altar is based in faith. When faith is weak or absent, we cannot perceive the love the unseen God and the risen Jesus have for us; therefore we cannot return it.

This came home to me one day when I was talking with a couple who were asking why their children didn't like to go to Mass. The husband had a simple answer: "They're lazy." His wife disagreed: "They're good kids, but they get nothing out of the Mass. They tell me that they pray just as well or better in their rooms."

By admitting that they prayed the young people acknowledged that they believed in God. But what kind of God? The impersonal, universal Other who exists someplace and may or may not be interested in human beings? The God of majesty ruling from a heavenly throne? The amorphous God to whom all religions can pay homage? Or the God who revealed an infinite love through Jesus and in Jesus? Faith in Jesus and in the community of believers is the basis for offering a gift of love when we gather to remember what Jesus has done for us.

To get to the heart of the meaning of the Mass, the first questions we should ask, it seems to me, are questions about our faith. What do we really believe about Jesus, about the importance of his life, death, resurrection and ascension in our lives? Then we can ask about the love we have for Jesus and the Father, the love which we try to show both in words and in deeds. Only then can we ask questions about the meaning of the Mass in our lives.

For Reflection and Sharing

1) Look deeply into your mind and heart. What do you really believe about Jesus and the importance of his death and resurrection for you? Write your conclusions in your own words.

2) Reflect on what the word *love* means to you and especially on what it means in your relationship with God. How do you express this love of God in word and in deed?

3) What images and ideas do the words "the sacrifice of the Mass" bring to your mind?

4) How do you show in your daily life that you have been to Mass on Sunday?

5) Prepare four gifts to give your Father at the next Mass you attend:

   —a sin to offer at the Penitential Rite

   —a need which will express your trust during the Opening Prayer

   —something you have done for another to present with the bread and wine

   —something for which you want to give thanks at the Prayer After Communion.

CHAPTER NINE

'In Memory of Me':
The Mass as a Ritual Meal

I like to have flowers in my room all the time. Sometimes someone brings me a plant or a bouquet, but it is usually a long time between gifts. I know that if I really want to have flowers all the time, the best thing I can do is plant my own garden.

Something similar is true about the Mass. I can wait for that wonderfully meaningful celebration which occurs now and then, or I can work with my interior garden so that flowers blossom whenever I attend the Eucharistic liturgy.

The first step in cultivating a garden is always to prepare the ground. In this case, that means to examine and perhaps change the way we view what is going on at the altar. Our *vision* of the ritual and its meaning determines both what we expect to get out of the Mass and what we bring to it. For, whether we realize it or not, our underlying vision affects everything we do.

The paradigm (or model) for this phenomenon is this: *vision* produces *attitudes* which in turn determine the *actions* we take and the *skills* we develop. The way we see a situation, the ideas we have about it—our vision—give rise to our attitudes. Attitudes are habitual ways of thinking which color, like tinted glasses, the way we see reality. The way we see reality, of course, will determine the decisions we make and the actions we take. These, in turn, will determine the skills we choose to develop.

Let me illustrate this model from a story in the *Los Angeles Times* about a Christian Coptic family who has left Egypt because of persecution by the Muslims. The article states their vision of

69

life: "Their lives focus on a strong nuclear family rooted in common religious beliefs." They see family and religion as core. This vision shapes their attitudes, how they see the world and how they make sense out of what goes on around them.

For example, the mother of the family says, "At work I might tell my friends about a problem my husband and I might have, and they just tell me to leave him because life is too short for problems." She finds this attitude astounding because, "In the Orthodox Coptic religion, divorces are granted only under the most extreme conditions and even then may lead to excommunication. I am different. I know in my mind that we are not going to have a divorce. So I know that any problems we have we will have to fix."

This attitude determines the way she and her husband work out their differences. The article does not say *how* they work out their problems, but they do not go to the divorce court.

Once we become conscious of this paradigm we know where to look for a way to change some aspect of our thinking or behavior. We may have to change our vision or view of the situation so that our attitudes will change. From a changed attitude new and different modes of action will emerge and we will develop new skills.

The Alcoholics Anonymous program is a fine illustration of working for change in actions by shifting one's vision, one's way of seeing reality. I have sat in the office hour after hour with men who have a problem with drink. Invariably, they say at first that they can handle their liquor, that they are not alcoholic. All they want is a little help, such as taking the pledge to give them some support. It isn't till they change their picture of themselves, their vision, and admit that they are powerless over alcohol and that their lives are unmanageable that any progress can be made.

They also have to see that a Power greater than themselves can restore them to sanity. From this new viewpoint flows an attitude of surrender of their lives to that Higher Power. This attitude helps them do things which they had not been able to do by themselves: staying sober 24 hours at a time, making reparation to people they have wronged, praying and meditating to improve their conscious contact with God.

Another simple way to see how the paradigm works is to imagine what you would say and do if you pulled into the garage and noticed that the new power mower was missing. If your basic way of seeing the situation (your vision) was that a thief had broken into the garage and taken the mower, your attitude would probably be anger and outrage, and your action to call the police. But suppose you discovered that your teenager had taken the mower to oil it and prepare it for use. Your feelings and attitudes would change instantly because you would see the situation in a new light—and you certainly would not call the police.

What does all this have to do with the Mass? Well, if we see the Mass as a time when the priest, the choir and the congregation are supposed to deliver flowers to us, we set ourselves up for disappointment. If, on the other hand, we see the Mass as a garden we plant and cultivate and take responsibility for, we will gather blossoms whenever we participate.

A Vision of the Mass

Each of us has a vision of the Mass, a personal understanding of what is occurring at the altar. From this personal vision flow our attitudes and our actions when we gather with the community. Our vision, however, may be limited; it certainly is conditioned by our past experiences.

Reflecting on the Church's vision of the Eucharist may expand our vision. The bishops gathered at the Second Vatican Council said in *The Constitution on the Sacred Liturgy*:

> At the Last Supper, on the night he was betrayed, our Savior instituted the Eucharistic Sacrifice of his Body and Blood. He did this in order to perpetuate the sacrifice of the Cross throughout the centuries until he should come again, and so to entrust to his beloved spouse, the Church, a memorial of his death and resurrection: a sacrament of love, a sign of unity, a bond of charity, a paschal banquet in which Christ is consumed, the mind is filled with grace and a pledge of future glory is given to us. (#47)

A lot is packed into that paragraph. Every word is important, but the key word is *memorial*. The community gathers to *remember* what Jesus did for it. This remembering is more than

71

calling an event to mind, like the signing of the Declaration of Independence on July 4th or the fact of our birth on our birthday. It is a *ritual* act by which we, as a remembering community, in some mysterious way *make present* Jesus' death on the cross and his resurrection, and thereby enter into—become a part of—that saving act.

When Jesus told his apostles, "Do this in memory of me," he was speaking as a Jew of his time. To the Jews, the ritual celebration of great religious realities was more than ceremony, altogether different from flying a flag and sounding Taps on Memorial Day. The celebration of a feast such as the Passover was a way of making the event commemorated present *now*.

Each person sitting at the Passover meal became part of the little band of Hebrew slaves taking flight from Egypt. Even though the actual Exodus was separated by a thousand years from the meal, each person at the table with Jesus personally experienced God's love and care as well as the gift of freedom. Thus Jesus was telling his apostles that when they broke bread in memory of his last meal, they would likewise be making present his life and death, resurrection and ascension. In and through that life we are saved, and in the Mass this salvation comes to fruition in our lives.

Ritual, then, is a way of penetrating and touching those tremendous realities which cannot adequately be put into words. It takes us beyond the senses—beyond what we can see, hear, feel or touch—to that which is deeper and more real. In the Mass that which is real but impossible to express adequately in words, that which is real but not seen at the altar, that which is real but not felt or fully comprehended—that reality is the mysterious something we call salvation. We are getting in touch with Jesus who by his life, death, resurrection and ascension has in some way "saved" us and "reunited" us with God.

Our Vision of Jesus

Going back to our paradigm, we cannot understand our attitudes toward the Mass without asking what our vision of Jesus is. Not merely what have we been taught about him, but what do we really believe about him? Belief is what forms our attitudes toward him and moves us into some sort of response to him and to his words.

We have to ask ourselves whether, in the deepest part of our being, we actually believe that Jesus is truly a human being like us and at the same time the Son of God. We have to ask ourselves whether we believe that Jesus' life, death, resurrection and ascension mean something to us. We may have to ask whether we feel a need to be "saved."

If our vision sees Jesus as both human and divine, we will have a different attitude toward him than if we believe that he is merely human. If we feel that we are in control of our lives and that we can work things out by ourselves, we will have a different attitude than if we really feel a need to be saved from our weaknesses and our sins.

I fully believe that one reason some Catholics have given up going to Mass is that, in their hearts, they do not feel a need for *salvation*, whatever that word means to them. They may be able to give the textbook answers about human need and the nature of salvation, but the answers which would come from personal conviction would be different.

I realize that the words I have just used are religious jargon, language which is totally inadequate to express the reality we celebrate and memorialize. This language is well-worn; it carries so many different connotations that it does not come as good and exciting news anymore. It has been around for 2,000 years. We are not hearing it for the first time, or hearing it proclaimed with enthusiasm and excitement. As adults, we often hear it with the ears of schoolchildren, because we have not heard more adult explanations of those realities, because we have not explored beyond childish imagination and understanding.

Until this shopworn language takes on some strong personal meaning for us, however, until we have made the plunge of faith into the unknown and the unknowable and cried out, "Lord, I do believe, help my unbelief," the Mass is not going to mean much to us. At best our vision of it will be askew. We will see it merely as a time of prayer or as a time to get a message about how to live our lives.

The vision of the Mass as a memorial ritual calls for an attitude of surrender in faith to Someone beyond us, an attitude of awe in the presence of mystery, an attitude of wonder and gratitude—and an attitude of joy and attentiveness to one another. In former times, the taking of holy water, the genuflections, the kneeling, the silence, the ringing of bells, the incensing, the recitation of the prayers in Latin, the solemn singing of Gregorian Chant—all these actions flowed from attitudes engendered by a vision of the Mass as the "mystery of faith." Externally, at least, they fostered a posture of reverence (though that reverence was not life-giving unless it expressed the personal conviction of individuals).

But the vision of the Eucharist as a ritual perpetuation of the sacrifice of the cross until Jesus comes again is only a partial vision. This vision in days gone by was stressed almost to the exclusion of an equally important vision: the Eucharist as the paschal banquet in which Christ himself is consumed. Seen in this way, the Eucharist is a sign of unity, a bond of charity and a pledge of future glory.

A Banquet

The Eucharist is a meal, a banquet—even though the altar seldom looks like our dining room table, even though we seldom gather around the altar as we do around the dinner table, even though the bread does not look like or taste like our common daily bread. The host's clothes, the dishes, the decorations do not readily conjure up an image of a Christmas or Thanksgiving meal. But again, we must remember that the Mass in which we are participating is not like a play on a stage; it does not try to recreate an actual banquet scene. It is a *ritual* meal, a stylized presentation in gesture and word which reaches out to the intangible and makes it present in our lives.

If we want to know what is made real by this meal we need only read the words St. John puts into Jesus' mouth at the Last Supper in his Gospel (John 14—17). Two sentences of that section sum up Jesus' life and death and tell what the Eucharist is all about:

"The command I give you is this,
that you love one another." (15:17)

and

"I pray also for those who will believe in me through
their [the Apostles'] word,
that all may be one

as you, Father, are in me, and I in you...." (17:20-21)

This banquet is a celebration of the fact that we have all been brought together into one family by Jesus—whether we know it or not, whether we feel it or not, whether we like it or not. It expresses our unity with Jesus, with the Father, with the Holy Spirit *and* with one another. It recalls not only the Last Supper, but also the good enriching things we have done together. It celebrates not only Jesus' love for us, but also our love for one another.

This banquet dimension of our vision of the Mass calls for attitudes which can be strikingly at variance with those engendered by the vision of the Mass as a memorial of the *sacrifice* of Jesus. It calls for an attitude of friendliness to all who gather to celebrate, whether we know them or not. (The common complaint that the parish is a cold place shows how little this attitude blossoms in many places.) This vision calls for a festive attitude, one of joy and excitement. This attitude requires us to pray and sing together. It calls for contact with our fellow banqueters, talking with them, greeting them, getting to know them, shaking hands with them. Who could enjoy a holiday meal at which everyone sits silently with eyes downcast?

At a banquet there is food, and the food at the paschal meal is Jesus himself. When I was ordained 40 years ago, we estimated that 65 percent of the people in church seldom received Holy Communion. Several years in a row I asked the ushers to count the house on Christmas and Easter, and also the people at the altar rail. Even on those days the number of communicants did not reach 50 percent of those present.

Today I would guess that a good 90 percent of the people receive Communion—even if they only step into church two or three times a year. They may be living together without benefit of clergy, they may be divorced and remarried several times, they may have just left the breakfast table—but they approach the altar. I can not judge their motives or ask them questions when they extend their hand and ask for the Lord. If they do so with a real conviction that they are receiving the Lord, I rejoice; because he came for the sick, not for the well, for sinners rather than for saints. If they do so merely because everyone else is doing it, I pity them; because they are missing the point of what we are doing.

Each time the priest or Eucharistic minister says, "The body of Christ," and we answer, "Amen," we are challenged to examine our vision of what we are eating. We can have very different ideas of what that simple phrase means. Our personal concept may be that the bread and wine are a sign of our fellowship with the others in the church, or that they are a symbol of Jesus, something that reminds us of him. Our personal vision may be that, in some way which we do not understand, Jesus is present in the bread and wine, or that they are no longer actually bread and wine but the person of Jesus. Our vision will determine our attitudes; our attitudes will determine the frequency with which we receive as well as the preparation and thanksgiving we make.

The faith of the Church says that the bread and wine become the actual person of Christ. Theologians argue about how this occurs, but *how* it occurs is not important. *That* it occurs is important. In faith we see beyond the appearances of bread and wine. We see Christ and examine the consequences of this faith vision in our lives.

'Who Do You Say I Am?'

Every time we receive Communion we are challenged to reexamine who we believe Jesus Christ to be. Any Catholic will say that Jesus Christ is "the Son of God" or "God and man." Dig further and you will find some interesting variations of that belief. It is not uncommon to find people who identify Jesus with God so totally that they forget or neglect his humanity. They think of Jesus as the all-powerful, all-knowing God, not really human like the rest of us. They do not believe that he really experienced all the things we humans must go through.

At the other end of the spectrum we find people who think of Jesus only as a man, a historical character who lived and died as we all do. They admit he was a great teacher, a dedicated leader, a prophet, a saint. They may go as far as to say that the godlikeness which is in all of us shone through his humanity in the most perfect way possible. But they believe that when he died he stayed in the grave as do all other human beings. Still others believe that Jesus "lost" his humanity when he rose and that he now is a mysterious spirit or power somewhere up in heaven.

Even when people say Jesus is truly God and truly human, each may have a different image of his humanity in mind. The Gospels present a many-faceted Jesus, and each of us has a predilection for one or the other of these images: the infant son of Mary, the Messiah, the teacher, the healer, the miracle-worker, the prophet, the man of suffering, the lawgiver, the judge, the friend of sinners, our brother, the risen Lord. Our predominate picture of him will affect our attitude at Mass, just as our attitude and feelings are affected by whether we are in the presence of a judge, of a friend, a teacher, a doctor. In each of these circumstances we speak differently; we carry ourselves differently; we expect different things from the other.

Our favorite image of Jesus may change when our needs change. One time we may need the healer, another time the forgiver, a third time the friend or judge. The Mass will mean more to us when we are clear about the Jesus we are approaching, the Jesus we will receive in Communion.

Jesus, Our Food

It is easy to see why Jesus told his friends to *eat* this bread and *drink* this cup. The food we ingest becomes one with us; in a very real sense we become what we eat. Jesus is the bond of unity between us and our fellow Christians. He is God's love for us made visible. He is the pledge of our future life.

But eating his body and drinking his blood does not automatically make us kind, loving, caring people. It does not automatically make us one with our fellow Christians. It does not automatically make us holy. Our attitudes are like the acids in our stomach which break down food so we can assimilate it. Our openness to other people, our desire for unity, our willingness to help and be identified with them, our willingness to forgive unconditionally, our surrender to God and our willingness to put our lives completely in his hands—these things make it possible for Jesus to be for us what the Council document said: a sacrament of love, a sign of unity, a bond of charity, a source of grace, a pledge of future glory.

For Reflection and Sharing

1) What are the "flowers" you would like others to give you at Mass? Check off the items which you think would help you get more nourishment from the Sunday Liturgy. These categories are not rigid or absolute. Your preferences will change with many circumstances, but check what you would like to find at the Sunday celebration *at this time:*

- ☐ more people whom I know and who are friendly
- ☐ a good choir which does most of the singing
- ☐ a lot of congregational singing
- ☐ no choir, no singing
- ☐ Latin or classical hymns and music
- ☐ popular or folk music
- ☐ prayers and ceremonies exactly the same all the time
- ☐ something unusual (dance, different prayers, clowns, etc.)
- ☐ a certain amount of variety but not enough to distract
- ☐ a very short homily or none at all
- ☐ a very dramatic and powerful preacher
- ☐ a homily which teaches us something about our faith
- ☐ a homily which tells how I am to live
- ☐ a homily which encourages and affirms me
- ☐ no one on the altar but the priest and the altar boys
- ☐ altar girls and more female ministers
- ☐ women priests
- ☐ lay ministers functioning on the altar
- ☐ exchanging the kiss of peace with the people close to me
- ☐ no kiss of peace
- ☐ getting out of the pew and moving around for the kiss of peace
- ☐ periods of quiet reflection
- ☐ something happening all the time
- ☐ a short (20- to 25-minute) Mass
- ☐ a Mass which may last an hour or longer
- ☐ a Mass with a small group of people I know well
- ☐ a Mass in a parish church with a large crowd of people
- ☐ a home Mass
- ☐ other (please specify)

2) To become more conscious of how the vision-attitudes-action model works in your life, think of two different jobs you have had, two different schools you have attended or two different people you have known. Pick one situation or person you liked very much and one you disliked or even hated.

> —Recall your *vision* at the time: How did you see each person or situation?

> —What *attitudes* toward each grew out of that vision?

> —How did your *actions* reflect your attitudes?

Now recall a change of *attitude* (for better or for worse) toward a person or situation. What change in your *vision* sparked the change? How did your *actions* change?

3) Reflect on what you think is happening when priest and people gather to celebrate the Eucharist. Do not describe the actions or list your expectations, but try to put into words what you think the ritual is all about, what it means. Do not give textbook answers, but give your *personal vision*.

Next, identify your *attitudes* toward what is going on.

Finally, decide how what you *do* during Mass is a result of your vision and your attitudes.

PART THREE

Getting More
Out of the Mass

CHAPTER TEN

Helping Ourselves:
Some Things to Try

At this point in our dialogue you may well ask, "All right, my friend, what you have said is interesting, but how do I get something more out of the Mass?" That's a fair question. I admit that my answer is yet incomplete even for me; it is an answer with which I am sure many of my friends will disagree. But I hope that my answer may help you find *your* answer.

The first thing I have to say is that the Mass makes sense precisely because it does not make sense. We can begin to understand it only when we admit we cannot understand it. The Mass is not just what it appears to be. If it were only prayers, songs and readings, a homily, eating a tiny wafer, then it would not be the Mass. If we grasp the meaning of the prayers, are inspired by the homily and touched by the songs, we have had a powerful, meaningful experience, but that experience is too small, too limited to contain the reality of what has actually occurred.

The Mass is like Ansel Adams's photographs of the mountains in Yosemite National Park: They are beautiful and awe-inspiring, but fall far short of standing on the park floor and seeing with more than the physical eye the size, the color, the texture, the feel of majestic Half Dome and Bridal Veil Falls.

To appreciate the Mass we have to allow the artist and the poet in each of us to see on the altar more than the eye can see, to hear inaudible sounds from long ago, to touch a body, a person, who cannot be felt. To appreciate the Mass we have to unbar the doors of rigid reason and allow the *mystic* in each of us to lead us into mysterious byways we do not comprehend. Many years ago G.K. Chesterton said it better than I can in his book *Orthodoxy*:

> Mysticism keeps men sane. As long as you have mystery you have health; when you destroy mystery you create morbidity. The ordinary man has always been sane because the ordinary man has always been a mystic. He has permitted the twilight. He has always had one foot in earth and the other in fairyland. He has always let himself free to doubt his gods; but (unlike the agnostic of to-day) free also to believe in them. He has always cared more for truth than for consistency. If he saw two truths that seemed to contradict each other, he would take the two truths and the contradiction along with them. His spiritual sight is stereoscopic, like his physical sight: He sees two different pictures at once and yet sees all the better for that. Thus he has always believed that there was such a thing as fate, but such a thing as free will also. Thus he believed that children are indeed the kingdom of heaven, but nevertheless ought to be obedient to the kingdom of earth. He admired youth because it was young and age because it was not. It is exactly the balance of apparent contradictions that has been the whole buoyancy of the healthy man. The whole secret of mysticism is this: that man can understand everything by the help of what he does not understand. The morbid logician seeks to make everything lucid, and succeeds in making everything mysterious. The mystic allows one thing to be mysterious, and everything else becomes lucid.

With one eye, our "stereoscopic spiritual sight" takes in the church building, the people, the paintings, the processions, the priest, the altar. With the other eye it sees a long-ago banquet table surrounded by 13 men, a loaf of bread, a cup of wine, a broken body hanging on a cross, blood streaming from a pierced heart, a cowed group of people locked in a room and a mysterious figure suddenly standing in their midst.

With one ear our stereoscopic spiritual hearing listens to

84

the singing, the words of the priest, the prayers of the congregation. The other ear hears words spoken long ago: "Love one another....Be one as my Father and I are one....This is my body. This is my blood. Do this in memory of me....Father, into your hands I commend my spirit....Peace be to you....It is I; be not afraid....It is expedient that I leave you...."

The rigid logician in us wants order and demands plausible explanations for everything the eye sees and the ear hears. The mystic in us says, "Be quiet. Enjoy what you do not understand as well as what you do understand. If the visible, the audible, the tangible bring you no joy, if they make no sense, if they bore you, remember that they are only the shell. The reality lies in what you do not see, hear or touch, in the mysterious something Jesus does today as he did 2,000 years ago."

At this point you may legitimately ask if this is the way *I* feel when I celebrate Mass. Seldom, to be honest—but frequently enough to know it is possible even when my experience is flat.

One time when I did experience the meaning of the Mass most powerfully was at the funeral of my brother, who was killed in a commercial plane crash. The airline flew me to Idaho to bury him. The night before the funeral all the priests I lived with in Chicago unexpectedly arrived to be with me and the family. Next morning at Mass they stood around the altar with me. The church was filled with friends and acquaintances. The casket was carried up the aisle while four trumpeters played a Bach chorale. The homily was a warm tribute from my brother's close priest-friend. I could barely voice the prayers for the lump in my throat; when tears closed my eyes, a friend on either side touched my arm in comfort.

I *knew* Calvary that day. When I said, "This is my body; this is my blood," my inner cry was, "My God, my God, why have you forsaken me?" I knew that we were celebrating something more than the end of one short life. I knew that the mysterious dimensions of my life, his life, his wife's and children's lives, the lives of everyone in that church were somehow caught up into the life, death and resurrection of Jesus, and that hope for something beyond the grave was more than an illusion.

What I experienced that day was also experienced by

many of the people in the church. As I was walking down the street the next day, a man my brother knew stopped me and said, "Reverend, I don't know how to say this. Don't be offended, but that was the best damn funeral I've ever been at." The mystic, the poet in him had been loosed for a moment; he too had experienced that mysterious unknown which makes sense out of what seems to be nonsense.

The fact that reason does not make clear the mystery of the Mass need not keep us from being as reasonable as we reasonably can be. As part of my answer to your presumed question, I will share with you some practical steps which have helped me realize that the Mass is indeed relevant in my life. But, first, I have to say something about my view of religion.

What Is Religion?

I admit that for many years my idea of religion was that it was a complex of laws, regulations, duties and prayers to which I had to be faithful. My God during those years was a gentleman, a person of dignity and honor, justice and faithfulness who could be counted upon to keep his part of any contract. I pictured him as an English gentleman, impeccably dressed with bowler hat, cane and spats, very proper and polite, dignified and remote. We would touch our hats in greeting as we passed each other and say the polite thing, each knowing and keeping his place.

But then two things happened which smashed that household idol which I had enshrined as my personal God.

The first was a talk by Father James Burtchaell, C.S.C., which later became a chapter in *Philemon's Problem: The Daily Dilemma of the Christian* under the title "The Father of Jesus, and Strange Gods Before Him." Jim expounded on the vision of the Father which Jesus presented in the story of the Prodigal Son. As he spoke of the implications of that vision for morality, for understanding the sacraments, for religious education, I felt hammer blow after hammer blow striking the idol I had called God. Gone was my gentleman God. Suddenly the poet, the mystic in me responded to a doting, loving Father who really cares for me more than I care for myself, who understands me better than I understand myself, who forgives me more easily than I forgive myself.

The second thing which changed my vision of God and thereby affected my appreciation of the Mass was a talk by Father Vincent Dwyer, O.C.S.O., on prayer. He quoted an old abbot who said that we pray best when we do not know we are praying, and then explained how our whole life can be a prayer. That talk broke the communication barrier between me and that loving Father of whom Burtchaell had spoken. No longer did I feel that I had to say the breviary and other formal prayers in order to be praying. The poet and mystic in me began to listen to the voice of God in the multitude of little daily events through which God reveals himself, and my response to those events was in a true sense my prayer.

As a result of those two talks and of subsequent study, reflection and prayer, I now see religion in a much different way. It is no longer something set apart, a special compartment of my daily living. It is synonymous with life.

Some people use religion as a justification for their self-righteousness. For others it smacks of magic: They expect ritual to manipulate God into action on their behalf. Still others see it as a way to avoid life by living a "supernatural" life, a life concerned only with a coming world. To live this religion is to live in a two-storied world where God, the soul and the spiritual operate out of the second story while daily life, relationships, work, politics and economics hold shop on the first floor.

For me the life of the world to come is a continuation of the life that is now; the natural and the supernatural are one unified whole in me and in my daily actions. I can no more divide the religious from the secular, the natural from the supernatural, than I can divide my body from my soul, my thoughts from my mind, my experiences from myself. For me religion is being conscious that my Father and I are making our way as best we can through the million and one little things that come up hour by hour: my work, my meals, my joys, my sorrows, my relationships, my prayers.

That view of life and religion has been most helpful for me in appreciating the Mass. In a very real sense I see the time spent at Mass as a time when I am *least* religious. It is a time taken out of my daily routine to sit back and review my religious activities, the myriad small actions which make up my day. It is a time to seek guidance for the day which is beginning. It is a time to be refreshed not by what is going on around me, but by what is going on within me.

Practical Suggestions

I have found four practices which help me use my time at Mass effectively, both when I am the celebrant and when I sit in the pews. I wish I could say that I practice them every day, but often I do none of them. On a good day I try two of them; on a super day, three. Nonetheless, each helps; so I offer them to you.

1) *Give yourself time.* Get to church ahead of time so you do not feel rushed and harried when Mass begins. Take a few minutes to calm the inner turmoil, to shut out pressing external activities, to collect your thoughts and to open yourself to the presence of God.

In the seminary we went to chapel at 5:30 a.m. for morning prayers and a half hour of meditation before the 6:30 Mass. I felt that this regimen was cruel and unnatural punishment inflicted on a growing boy who needed his sleep. I always got up at the last minute, rushed into chapel and promptly dozed off with my eyes open.

Then came the parish. No more getting to bed by 10:00 p.m.; most of the time I was lucky to make it by midnight. But I still had to be up for the 6:30 Mass. The alarm rang at 6:10, giving me just enough time for a shower (thank heavens I did not have to blow-dry my crewcut) and a quick shave before I jumped into my clothes and rushed into the sacristy. The routine didn't change if I had the 7:00 or 7:30 Mass: Get up, get dressed, dash to church.

Just recently I have discovered that if I get up and get started 15 minutes earlier, I do not lose any needed sleep. I gain a few quiet minutes to gather my thoughts, quiet my mind and rouse my consciousness of the presence of God before Mass. Even with this preparation, I sometimes arrive at the altar with sleep in my eyes and a million distracting thoughts clamoring for my attention. But when I do arrive recollected and at peace, I can sense the mysterious, the something beyond what I can see and hear, and my day is the better for it.

2) *Read ahead.* Take a look at the prayers and readings before you come to church. I have found that reading the Scripture lessons the night before or even a half hour *before* Mass

focuses my thoughts *during* Mass. When the biblical readings come at me cold and fast, I cannot quickly put them into the context of my life. At best I recall a few scholarly insights. I have to mull over a passage before I find its message for me. But once that message is clear, hearing the Scripture repeated at Mass gives all the prayers and actions of the liturgy its patina.

There is an ancient saying that the law of prayer is the law of belief, and that the law of belief is the law of prayer. In other words, what we believe will be expressed in our prayers; what we say in our prayers will form our beliefs. When we take the time to read the prayers of the Mass ahead of time we have the opportunity to reflect on what they mean and how they express what we do believe. The words then take on personal meaning and at the same time form and strengthen our beliefs.

Recently I read an article in *Chicago Studies* which might be helpful in preparing for Mass and especially for giving the Scripture readings a personal touch. Author Ted Guzie says that, when Jesus told his apostles, "Do this in memory of me," he was telling them to repeat not only what he did at the Last Supper, but also to repeat and recall all that he had told them and all that he had done at previous meals with them. This feeding at the table of remembrance was to be not only with bread, but also with word and ritual action.

The apostles remembered how Jesus had reached out to sinners and society's outcasts at a meal in Levi's house (Luke 5:27-39). What Jesus had done in person his followers were to do in a healing and reconciling event, the memory meal. The apostles recalled the meal at which the woman of the city had expressed her love for Jesus and how he had accepted it and forgiven her (Luke 7:36-50). The commemoration meals were likewise to be expressions of forgiveness, of love for Jesus and for one another. They recalled that he had blessed Zacchaeus for restoring any ill-gotten gains and pledging half his possessions to the poor (Luke 19:1-10). If their future meals were truly to remember what the Lord had done, they and all Christians would have to share with the needy.

In the years to come the community remembered that Jesus had spoken the parables on forgiveness at a meal (Luke 15:1-32), and that he had commended Mary for sitting at his feet and listening while Martha kept busy (Luke 10:38-42). The meals the apostles had shared with Jesus had been moments of real fellowship when love was celebrated, hurts forgiven, the poor and outcasts cared for, unity restored. The meal celebrated in memory of Jesus was to recall all those times and bring them into the life of the community.

But at the Mass we remember more than the meals Jesus had with his friends; we recall his entire life. As we prepare the Gospel ahead of time and listen to it read at the liturgy, our vision informs us that what Jesus did then, he is doing now. Somehow we are the sinner being healed and reconciled. Our love is being accepted, our gift, however small, is being praised. We are the people being healed, being taught, being sent. The Mass is the time when the risen Lord does in our midst what he did in first-century Palestine. It is a time when we celebrate table fellowship with Jesus and with all his followers down through the centuries.

3) *Use your missalette*. I know this recommendation will get me in trouble with my closest associates and with most liturgists. They think following the readings in the missalette is a distraction rather than a help.

A recent article in a magazine for priests stated quite correctly that the liturgy is sacred drama. Working from this premise, the author concluded, "With the sense of hearing we can apprehend far more than a message in the voice of the speaker. We hear the speaker's personal conviction that the message is true. There is also a message for the sense of sight in the way the lector is dressed and uses his body at the lectern, in the way the book is handled and incensed."

Just as I feel energy flow into me from a congregation which is alive and attentive, so too there is a subtle interaction between a good reader and the congregation. One such reader says, "When I read, I know I've done well when the folks out there *drop* their missalettes and listen not just to the Word, but to what it means to me."

I personally agree with all this, but unfortunately I seldom find all these wonderful messages coming through to me. In fact, the message often enough is just the opposite because of the poor diction or sloppy stance of the lector. We live in a flawed world in which poorly endowed or badly trained readers murder not only the English language but the Word of God as well.

I often find it most difficult to pay attention to a person

reading the Scriptures when I am the celebrant at the liturgy. Poor diction, mispronounced words, clumsy phrasing, lifeless tone or poor acoustics throw a switch, and my mind races down another track. It is not unusual for me to get up and read the Gospel without the foggiest idea of what the first two readings were all about unless I was following them in a lectionary or in a missalette. In the absence of well-trained, very devout lectors, I suggest that people follow along in the missalette and at least read the message.

McMaster and Grinder point out a further gain in their book *Precision: A New Approach to Communication*:

> We obtain information through our senses. That is we see, hear and feel things and events. We also represent or store these experiences in similar ways. We have the ability to recall pictures, sounds and feelings just as they happened or as we create them. . . . Most people develop favorite ways of representing the world and their experience. Some are primarily conscious of visual memory and representation, some of talking and sound and others of feelings. These are essentially the private maps or models of the world each of us creates. . . . These representational systems may be thought of as the way people think.

It seems obvious that people whose representational map is primarily visual will tune in most quickly to a message they see as well as hear and process it much more easily. Of course, these two senses work best together when the lector and the person following a missalette read at the same pace. If not, there is the danger the person using the missalette will finish more quickly and gaze off into space until the lector is finished. People whose respresentational map is primarily auditory may, of course, be better off simply listening.

If you find it difficult to follow the readings, and if following along in a missalette helps you keep your mind on the Scripture, do it. The important thing, it seems to me, is to open our spiritual ears to hear the stereoscopic sound of which Chesterton spoke, to hear words spoken here and now as the accompaniment for that mysterious melody which has played for 2,000 years and is ever new, fresh and alive.

4) *Don't come empty-handed*. To get something out of Mass

we have to bring something. We bring ourselves, of course, but what specifically about ourselves are we offering at this particular Mass?

Try offering the four gifts we talked about in Chapter Eight. Take a few minutes before Mass to prepare four specific gifts to be offered to the Father, through the Son, in union with the Holy Spirit: one specific fault or sin to lay before God for forgiveness; your trust manifested by asking for one thing; something you have done to share your bounty with others; thanksgiving for some one thing the Lord has done for you since the last time you celebrated the Eucharist.

Most of the time these four gifts will be small, but if they are very specific they will help us grasp in the depth of our being the connection between liturgy and our lives.

Remote Preparation

I admit that it is difficult to see in our ordinary Sunday Mass all those wonderful things encompassed in the Last Supper. We usually celebrate in a large building with hundreds of people who do not know one another—not a setting very conducive to a feeling of real table fellowship.

But large numbers are a fact of life. If we participate with large groups then we have to do something more to build up our personal memories. We have to become sensitive to the overtones which evoke a sense of healing, of unity, of sharing, of love. In other words, we need some sort of remote preparation for the Eucharist which will give meaning to the ordinary large Sunday celebration. For this reason I offer two suggestions, one from me and the other from Ted Guzie.

1) *Build up a store of memories* of fellowship at Mass, memories of gatherings with like-minded people, memories of healing and of sharing in small groups (such as a home Mass).

For instance, I celebrated Palm Sunday with a group of 20 or so Catholic Family Movement couples 35 years ago. On Friday night and all day Saturday we shared our dreams and frustrations. Then, on Sunday, we gathered in a very cold small chapel for the Palm Sunday service. My "altar boys" were men who hadn't served in years. They did everything with aplomb even though they went in different directions. We blessed the palms outdoors in a cold, bitter wind. The procession into church was as orderly as a group of survivors struggling home after an earthquake. The man who led the singing flatted even when he held one tone. (Someone remarked that the notes he sang were part of a tribal heritage not found in Western musical notation.)

In spite of all the confusion and cold, there was a warmth in that celebration which I still feel to this day. We were friends celebrating together. The same feeling has been nourished by other small-group Masses over the years. It comes back to me on Sundays when I look out over 600 or 800 people and see families or friends with whom I have celebrated in less formal, more intimate settings.

2) *Create your own experiences of table fellowship* as a foundation for participation in the Eucharist. Ted Guzie, in the article quoted on page 89, says: "To share a meal in peace and harmony is a great grace, one of God's most precious gifts to us. We are a sacred and precious people and that sacredness is not first celebrated in a large assembly. We need to recognize the gift a meal carries, accept it with awareness and so enjoy some of our meals in an atmosphere of thanksgiving and awareness."

On the face of it this seems like a dreamy-eyed idealist's suggestion. Many families rarely turn off the TV and sit down together for a meal. But I think enough families do eat together at least on big occasions to make it worthwhile.

Some time ago I gave a crystal goblet to a couple as a wedding present. We used it as a chalice at their wedding. They have since used it on special occasions. When I have dinner with them they bring it out, and we begin the meal with a simple prayer service like the one Guzie outlines in his article. That goblet is becoming associated with special occasions, friendship, prayer—an association which is an ideal preparation for participating on Sunday in the sacrament of unity and peace.

The simple ritual Guzie suggests could easily replace the usual blessing of the food; it takes only a few minutes:

—Set aside a special cup, a "blessing cup," for just such occasions. Fill it with wine or some other beverage everyone enjoys.

—Buy a loaf of bread—perhaps a special kind reserved for this occasion.

—Read a short passage from Scripture. (The Gospel for the coming Sunday would be perfect.) Then allow each person to share what the passage says to him or her.

—Give the people at the table time to offer petitions, express thanksgiving, sorrows or joys, or merely pray in silence.

—One person takes the "blessing cup" and blesses it. Guzie suggests this prayer: "Blessed are you, Father, for all the gifts you have given us. Blessed are you in Jesus, your Son and our brother, who was poured out for us." All drink from the one cup.

—One person blesses the bread: "Blessed are you, Father, for giving us bread to eat. Blessed are you in Jesus, your Son and our brother, who was broken for us. We recognize him and give you thanks in the breaking of bread." Then all eat a piece of the bread.

The Blessing Cup, by Rock Travnikar, O.F.M. (St. Anthony Messenger Press, 1979), offers 24 similar rituals for family use. Or a family can easily adapt or create a little ritual of its own. If such a ritual is used on joyous occasions and on sorrowful ones, at times when hurts are forgiven and when decisions are made to share with the needy, a family will gradually build a frame of reference which will enrich the flavor of the ritual Eucharistic meal.

The suggestions I have given may or may not help you. The most important thing they can do is to encourage you *frequently* to ask yourself what little thing you can do to make the Mass more relevant in your life. Sometimes reading what others do or asking others what they do helps. At other times, you will find your own ways. The important thing is to keep trying.

For Reflection and Sharing

1) Do a little exercise to see if you can release some of the poet, the mystic in you. Write a poetic description of someone you love. Describe the person's physical appearances or features, but describe them in words which express what that person means to you. Or tell what the person has done for you and with you, using words which are loaded with the meaning of these actions. Or merely tell in poetic and symbolic language what this person means to you.

Now go back over what you wrote and ask yourself:
   a) Does it adequately express the reality of that person and the relationship between you?

   b) Can you put into words—any words, no matter how many—the total reality of what exists between you and that person?

   c) Would a saying or a slogan be able to express all your feelings for that person?

If your answer to all three questions is no, you know why it is the poet and the mystic in you that must try to express what the Mass means to you.

2) Now reflect on your ideas of religion, especially on your images of God.
   a) When you were young, what was your image of God? What was your relationship to this God and how did you feel about him?

b) What is your image of God now? What is your relationship to God now, and how do you feel about the God you now worship? How do you define religion now? How does the Mass fit in with this relationship you feel you now have with God?

3) What are some things you do to make the Mass relevant for yourself?

4) What *one* thing can you do this week to prepare for the Sunday liturgy?

CHAPTER ELEVEN

A Place in the Story:
The Human Search for Meaning

A s I stand at the foot of the
sanctuary and distribute Communion at the 5 p.m. Saturday
Mass, I often wonder whether there will be enough people
coming 20 years from now to justify one lay minister of the
Eucharist, much less the five who now assist. The majority—the
vast majority—of faces in the long line that passes before me
bear the marks of 50 or more years of struggle. Young, fresh,
unlined faces are relatively few.

At times I comfort myself with the thought that older
people come to the anticipated Mass. But Sunday morning gives
lie to that theory. The picture is not much better at the 8:00 Mass
and only slightly better at the later Masses.

I ask myself how many of the young and middle-aged
adults who can find no pressing motive for approaching the
Lord's table will find such a reason later in life or will be able
to motivate their children to participate in the Eucharist on a
regular basis. I doubt they will do either.

It is rather easy to blame the spirit of the times—selfishness,
materialism, the breakdown of family and community—for
dwindling participation at Mass. It is too easy to accept dull
liturgies, boring sermons, cold and indifferent communities as
valid reasons for missing Mass. I know that most of the reasons,
both sociological and theological, which motivated the people
of my generation have little impact on people I talk to today.

It is very difficult for me to look for different and more
compelling reasons at this late age. The advice given centuries

ago to samurai warriors comes to mind as I make a stab at a reason which may help people today see the value of the Mass for themselves. The ancient Japanese sage said, "When crossing marshes, your only concern should be to get over them without delay. Take an arrow in your forehead, never in your back. Don't always think in a straight line."

We certainly are in a religious marsh, if not in a deep impenetrable swamp, and we will never get out of it if all we do is lament that we are in a quagmire of religious indifference, if we turn our backs on the challenge offered by people who ask what meaning the Mass has in their lives.

But it is the last bit of advice that intrigues me most. I do not see how thinking in a straight line—that is, explaining the origin, history and meaning of the prayers and parts of the Mass—will motivate people to regular and more intense participation. Scholars are intrigued by the history and the structure of the Mass, but I doubt whether many people are moved to rise and shine on Sunday morning by such information.

The Eucharist will only become vital and meaningful when we no longer approach it in a logical, intellectual, objective, analytical manner. Only when we look at it out of the side of our eye, when we approach it obliquely from another viewpoint, will we catch the brilliant gleam of its importance and meaning.

This idea, I admit, is new to me. I have always looked to the historical and theological aspects of the Eucharist for my own personal motivation. Only recently have I realized how unsatisfying that effort is. Straight-line thinking examines and explains the nature of sacrifice to a people unfamiliar with sacred groves and the smoke of burning flesh rising from temple altars. It tries to justify transubstantiation to a people with very scientific minds. It preaches the history of the Eucharist to people who live in a world which has changed more in the last five years than in all the years human beings have walked the earth. In other words, straight-line thinking concentrates on the objective reality of what is happening at the altar.

Thinking in something other than a straight line enables us to approach the Mass from other angles. For instance, we can ask what human needs the celebration of the Eucharist meets. In the prescientific age I suspect that the vast majority of people went to Mass because they needed some sort of physical help. They were sick, and there were few medicines, no wonder drugs, no CAT scans, no heart transplants. They had little control over their food supply: Drought meant famine; there was no transportation system to bring American wheat to Russian workers. Death was an ever-present threat to the young as well as to the old. Seventy-four was not an average life expectancy, but heroic achievement. Travel was dangerous; one literally took one's life in one's hands when starting on a journey of 50 miles.

In our society the need for God's intervention in these situations has diminished drastically. Droughts will affect nothing but the price of food on our table. Death can be pushed back till it becomes a longed-for relief from years of struggle. Technology promises miracles of healing and places far-flung corners of the world within easy reach.

I think we have to look more deeply at our real needs, needs which all people have but which often are not conscious or verbalized.

A 'Nonlinear' Answer

Recently I was asked, "Why go to Mass when there is no fellowship among the people, when the sermon is dull and when what is being said and done is boring?" My answer did not follow a straight line.

I said, "I go to Mass to find meaning in my life, to recall consciously a story of which I am a part." I know that those who do not make an effort to remember are doomed to forget. I need constant reminders of who I am as a person, as a Christian and as a Catholic. That kind of remembering is much more than knowing what religion to state on a form I am filling out. It is constant consciousness of my identity as I think and judge and act in thousands of little ways during the day.

I am not sure how clearly I can explain my above answer, but I will follow another bit of advice to the samurai warriors: "If you walk, just walk. If you sit, just sit. But whatever you do, don't wobble." I'll explain my reason as best I can.

One of the most basic human needs is to know who we are. We cannot function effectively or achieve any degree of contentment and happiness unless we know who we are—not merely our name, address and social security number, but who and what we are as human beings.

This need gives rise to three basic questions: *Who am I? Where did I come from? Where am I going?* It takes little experience and reflection to realize how important the answers to these questions are for each individual. Shallow, shortsighted, superficial answers may satisfy for a while, but there comes a time when people need and want ultimate answers.

A fourth question flows from those three: *How do I live a fulfilling life?* The gang member spray-painting graffiti on a wall as well as the financial wizard, the artist, the housewife, the butcher, the baker and the candlestick-maker all are trying to answer that question in some way or other. In their search for an answer, people look to heroes and villains who demonstrate appropriate or inappropriate behavior. Every time they think they have an answer, they are confronted by rebels, people who have values and ideals different from the conventional ones.

Still another question then arises: *Where can I look for help to live a fulfilling life?* Where can I find help in this threatening and confusing world? Very soon in life, whether or not we consciously avert to the fact, we realize that we are not in control of 99 percent of what happens to us and we begin looking for help. The baby realizes it can't feed itself, and the nuclear scientist realizes that he can't control the effects of his discovery.

In the movie *2001* a group of apes discover a mysterious black monolith in their midst and suddenly begin to manifest reason. They use bones as tools and weapons; before long speech develops. We know that with speech come stories. Before anyone recorded history, people created and told stories which attempted to answer the basic questions about life. It is precisely by knowing, accepting, remembering and entering into one such group of stories that we can look at the Mass in a nonlinear way.

This group of stories, the Judeo-Christian history of salvation, answers better than any closely reasoned, analytical or philosophical explanation the basic questions people are struggling with. For years we thought of the Bible, both Old and New Testaments, as God's book about God. In reality, those 72 books are God's book about human questions. By hearing these stories over and over again, by reflecting on them in the light of our ever-changing experience, we get a clearer picture of who we are, where we came from, where we are going, how we are going to get there and who will help.

The variety of these stories is as great as the many colors

of Joseph's coat. There are creation stories, stories of crises in the lives of individuals and of nations. There are value stories, stories of heroes and villains, stories of rebels who defied the conventional wisdom of their times. All these stories center on one outstanding personality, Jesus Christ, and on the people who prepared the way for him and who followed in his footsteps.

As these stories become more and more part of our thinking, we begin to see ourselves in an ever-expanding circle of relationships—until we realize that we are in relation to the ultimate reality. We begin to realize that our origin was not just in the meeting of a single sperm with a tiny egg, but in the infinite mind of God, and that our destiny is not the grave but something wonderful beyond the curtain which falls at death. We are assured that there is a benevolent power outside ourselves, directing, controlling and overcoming situations in which we need help and out of which we can make no sense. Our thinking becomes so permeated by the values in these stories and by the way Jesus thought and acted that we make these values our own and act in light of them. We know then who we really are.

If I see these stories merely as a record of events which happened long ago, an occasional telling is sufficient to keep them in my memory. But if they indicate the direction in which I am to search for the meaning of life, then I need to hear them over and over again as the circumstances of my life change. If they are to guide my life, help me form my self-image, satisfy my need for meaning and intelligibility, then they must be retold frequently—not only in words but also in action and ritual. They are the touchstones which help me see reality as it actually is, not as I think or hope it is.

At Mass these stories are told and interpreted time and time again in the Liturgy of the Word. But the retelling and interpretation, interesting and inspiring as it may be, is only one way in which the story is retold to me.

The Mass as Story

The liturgy itself is one long story, one long narrative dealing with my life. The Bible records only the first stages of an ongoing story of God's concern for his people. By sharing in

101

the liturgy, I have a part in that story; I give it flesh and blood right here and now. How that story worked out in the past and how it might work out in the future is interesting, but my real concern is how that story is unfolding today in my life.

To find meaning in the Mass, it seems to me, I have to approach the story being told by the liturgy with the openness of a child who says, time and time again, "Tell me about Goldilocks and the three bears." I want to hear the story of God's love for me over and over again, because I need to recognize that I actually do have a part in the divine plan unfolding in our times.

To have this vision, this mindset, two things are necessary. The first is to *know* the meaning, the purpose and the interpretation of the stories. The second is to *accept* the stories as answers to my basic questions about life. In other words, faith is needed—not so much belief in scriptural events as historical happenings, but acceptance of them as stories which pull together and express the Christian's view of self and life.

When I approach the Eucharist with this attitude, then I find help, relevance and meaning—not only in the Scriptures and in the homily, but also in all the other elements of the Mass. For example, the hymns and psalms contain endless allusions to who we are as individuals and as a people, to where we come from and where we are going, to whom we can turn for help in this confusing world. The prayers, while short and succinct, are explicit in their answers to these questions.

A prayer addressed to God as Father or as Lord, as Creator, Judge or Giver of gifts tells us a lot about who we are and why we are here. When we ask for peace, forgiveness, health, salvation, love and hope, the prayers echo our daily needs.

It is not enough for me to reflect once or twice a year that I need those things. I have to recall these needs at least weekly, if not daily. When we pray at Mass we not only recall God's love and concern for us, we also situate ourselves in that love and care operating here and now. We take stock of where we are, of what we need and from whom we hope to get it. We thank God for what he has done; we praise him for his power; we ask his help. We also make a commitment to face and fulfill the responsibilities arising from the fact that we are part of the ongoing story of God's involvement with us and with our world.

In the Mass this story unfolds not only in the readings and the homily, not only in the hymns and psalms, not only in the prayers, but also on a deeper, nonrational level in the action and ritual. Blessings, mixing of wine and water, breaking and sharing one bread, drinking from one cup, the sign of peace—all these communicate nonverbally the core elements of the story of who we are and why we are here.

Theologically we say that the life, death, resurrection and ascension of Jesus is made present, and we take part in it. When I am not bothered by scientific questions of how bread and wine can become the body and blood of Christ, and when I remember that he told us to do this in memory of him, I gradually become more and more conscious that I am loved unto death, that I can find the fullness of life which Jesus promised, that he is with me to free me from the bondage of fear and sin, that I can tap and use the power of the Spirit who resides in me.

I admit that these ideas are sketchy and need to be worked out in more detail. I admit that their full impact hits me only now and then. I admit that the Scriptures and the homilies have to be proclaimed in a much more convincing fashion. I admit that the prayers have to be said with more meaning and the actions performed in a more telling manner. Nevertheless, I am convinced that I find relevance, meaning, significance and importance in the Mass only when I take part in it with both mind and heart, with body and spirit. It is not enough for me to listen and pray, though that is important. I also have to open myself to the ritual, to the actions, to the symbols so that I come in contact with the story of God's loving concern for his people—and for me.

A Question of Identity

I began this book by saying that I am looking for a compelling reason for people to go to Mass today. As I come close to the book's end, I realize that I can't find one universally compelling reason for going to Mass. There are many good reasons for attending. Each of these will serve us well at different times in our lives, but I doubt whether one will suffice all our lives.

I can tell you that at times people go to get something out of the Mass. We look for help in a difficult situation; we look for inspiration; we look for fellowship. But I also know that getting something out of Mass is not a powerful enough motive for a lifelong practice because there always are dry periods. In this book I have suggested that concentrating on what *we bring to Mass* will help us find it more relevant in our lives, but again I must admit that this practice too becomes routine and loses its power to motivate. Individuals have personal motives for attending Mass—habit, a mystical experience, a longing for God—but these usually have little influence on other people.

I do know, however, that if I intend to belong to the community we call the Catholic Church, and if I intend to take that membership seriously as a way of life and not merely as a convenient label, I need to ritualize that identity time and time again, week after week, so that I remember who I am and to what I am committed.

A young man on whom I tried all these reasons said that perhaps he would have to wait until his world fell in and life's basic questions became important to him. At present he thought he knew who he was, what he wanted out of life and how he was to get it. Perhaps he has a point. People may have to wait till they feel the *need* for answers to these basic questions before they look seriously to the story and the ritual of the Mass for help.

For Reflection and Sharing

Perhaps the best way for you to get some idea of what I have been saying is to take the text—the entire text—of next Sunday's Mass and read it carefully, picking out words and phrases which seem to you to allude to or suggest answers to the questions: Who am I? Where do I come from? Where am I going? Who can help me on my journey? What do I need to do to get where I hope I am going?

When you have picked out the words and phrases and have written them down, pick two or three of them which seem to resonate most with the questions you are asking about life at this time. Spell out in five or six lines how they throw some light on your questions or on your situation.

CHAPTER TWELVE

Where Do We Go From Here?
Enriching the Experience

Working on this book for the
past six or eight months has been a great learning experience
for me. First, I had to make a real effort to find out why laypeople
still go to Mass.

Most of the people I questioned still go to Mass regularly;
they said they get a good deal out of participating even though
many of their children hardly ever darken a church door. Many
said they enjoyed the quiet time when they got away from all
distractions and had some time alone with God. Others saw it
as an occasion when they were inspired by the preaching and
the singing. A good many felt that they received help with the
problems of life. A few emphasized the reception of Communion
as the primary benefit. Few gave any clear-cut theological
reasons—even when they attended daily Mass. But all seemed
conscious through faith that something important to them and
for them occurs at the Eucharist.

My question invariably led to an array of complaints about
the way the liturgy is celebrated. Some of these, such as the
universal lament that many homilies are pious, boring platitudes
which in no way relate to life, seem justified. Others have a
touch of humor. One woman refuses to move from her spot or
extend the greeting of peace to the strangers around her because,
she says, "They shake your hand, but their eyes and the
expression on their faces show that they have no interest in you."

But something else came from these conversations. Again
and again people spoke of the good experiences they had had

at Mass. Most of the time these occurred when they participated in small group liturgies celebrated in an intimate, informal setting. Within a large parish a regular diet of these small gatherings is impossible. It does seem important, however, that people at some time or other have the opportunity to experience a home Mass or a Mass celebrated for a small group.

An ideal time for such small celebrations is at the conclusion of programs such as Renew, Genesis II, Marriage Encounter, Christ Renews His Parish, etc. During these programs the participants have shared at a rather deep level and have experienced a real sense of community. When this experience is capped by a Mass which draws on what occurred during the program, people find that the celebration of the Eucharist does relate to their lives. This discovery helps give meaning to the Sunday gatherings of the entire parish, especially when their new-found friends are present.

Some Simple First Steps

The second thing I had to do during these six months was to ask myself the question I asked others. When I asked myself why I go to Mass, my answers revealed that my motives are many and mixed. It has become clear to me that the explanations of the theologians, liturgists and spiritual masters are not as convincing as I thought and wished. Many purely human considerations enter in. These are good, but they need to be refined or purified. I am still seeking a completely satisfactory answer, but I am comforted by the words of an 80-year-old religious who said, "Teach the people it is all right to question and to doubt. Doubts are inevitable when we think and ask intelligent questions. Doubts do not destroy faith."

I have also had to ask myself how well I preside at the Eucharist and, as a result of trying to answer that question, I have made a few changes in my behavior. The role of the priest is not merely to "say Mass." He is to lead the congregation and help the people pray along with him. I realized that I couldn't ask the people to pray unless I myself was praying.

I had said the Mass prayers day after day for 40 years; for 25 of those years I had great difficulty understanding the words because they were in Latin. I had developed a bad habit of *reciting* the prayers rather than *praying* them. So I tried three simple things which—at least some of the time—help me feel that I am praying. These three practices are obvious and have been preached to me many times in retreats, but some of us need a bit of an earthquake to see the obvious.

First, I slowed down. No need to finish Mass in 15 minutes. Second, I began to put some inflection in my voice, some feeling in the words I was saying. Finally, I make an effort to be conscious that I am talking to someone who cares about me and who is important to me.

This is a form of behavior modification. I *act* as I know I should act if my words are to be prayers, and soon I find that I *am* praying.

Now it bothers *me* when the congregation hurries through the Gloria, the Creed or the Our Father in a monotonous, singsong manner without pause, inflection or feeling. I find that when we all slow down a bit, pause where it makes sense and speak with feeling (as if we were talking to someone we could see), then a sense of reverence and prayer flows through the church.

I find that I am making a real effort to speak directly to the people, as though I were talking one to one. At the beginning of Mass I try to be sincere in greeting the people, and I try to bring in a reference to the feast or to something of particular interest to the parish. When I ask the people to pray, I try to give them a few moments to do just that. I feel a tinge of electricity when the people answer sincerely and with feeling.

We all sense the difference between the perfunctory, "Hello, how are you?" which two acquaintances exchange as they pass in the street, and the sincere welcome with which close friends meet. Taking exchanges at Mass seriously, saying them with meaning and feeling, can do a lot to help us get more out of the Mass.

Sincere Gestures Can Help

I am convinced that the Mass will mean more to us not when brilliant innovations capture our imagination, but when our imagination puts feeling and meaning into the things we already say and do. For example, simple gestures done consciously and prayerfully can draw us into the Mass in a way that words cannot. How better to express our union in Christ than by holding hands with the people next to us during the Our Father? Blessing ourselves slowly with the Sign of the Cross helps us realize whom we are calling upon to be with us. If we sign ourselves on our forehead, lips and heart before the Gospel and ask God to let his Word penetrate our minds, pour forth from our lips and inflame our hearts, we are preparing ourselves to get something out of the reading and the homily rather than daring the celebrant to hold our interest.

These simple, obvious practices help me relax when I am at the altar. As a result I sense that my voice, my gestures are more sincere, warm, inviting. I also feel free to exercise the permissions in the sacramentary to use my own words and relate the parts of the Mass to the homily or to the particular occasion we are celebrating. In a word, I am beginning to enjoy presiding at the Eucharist, especially when the congregation responds with warmth and feeling.

Conclusion

I hope that these reflections of mine have helped you reflect on the way you participate at Mass. The degree of our participation and of our satisfaction will vary from time to time. There will be highs and lows in our feelings about the Mass—as there are in all relationships. Our relationship with God and with one another at the Eucharist cannot be judged solely in terms of the highs we have experienced. No worthwhile relationship always operates at a peak pitch.

Neither can we judge what the Mass means in our lives only by the lows. Every relationship has low points, some of which can be rather lengthy. The meaning of the Mass can only be judged by an overall evaluation of its effect on our life, on our prayers, on our faith, on our relationship to God, self and neighbors.

A true evaluation of the importance of the Mass for each of us is not easy to make. It is hard to see the overall picture. It is hard to judge the results. It is hard to be satisfied with small, imperceptible changes. Most of all, it is hard to travel in a desert where there seems to be no water anyplace.

For this reason I hope that I have raised a few basic questions for you. These questions will not lead you to pat, once-and-for-all answers. They will, however, point out a general direction in which to look for answers which satisfy you. The questions will keep coming back, time and time again. You will mostly find answers different from mine. But the questions themselves, I think, are basic to our identity as Roman Catholic Christians, basic to our relationship with ourselves, our neighbors and our God.

For Ongoing Reflection

Now that you have finished this book, there is still much to be done to make the Mass the source of your strength and the center of your life. Make it a habit frequently to question your motives and your ideas about what actually occurs at the Eucharist. Reading, discussions with your fellow Catholics and going back over the suggestions made at the end of each chapter in this book may help you with that questioning.

1) Each time you go to Mass, spend a few minutes beforehand asking yourself:

  a) Why am I going to Mass today?

  b) What does my faith tell me is about to occur at Mass?

  c) What do I have to bring to this Mass?

  d) What do I hope will happen in my life as a result of joining the community in celebrating the death and resurrection of Jesus?

Five or 10 minutes would suffice to answer these questions each week. If you wrote down your answers and in time added your own questions, reflections and insights, you very well might have a record of a progressive deepening of faith in the risen Jesus present and acting in the community which gathers to celebrate with him.